Pierce Brosnan

Peter Carrick has been writing professionally for most of his working life, as a journalist, music correspondent and columnist, public
relations consultant, ghost writer and author. His work, under his
own name and various pen names, has appeared in numerous publi-
cations in the UK and USA. He has specialized in music,
showbusiness and entertainment. Now the author of more than
thirty books, his celebrity biographies of Fred Astaire, Bob Hope,
Barbra Streisand, Liza Minnelli, Richard Gere and Mel Gibson are
all published in hardback by Hale. Peter Carrick was born in Hull
and now lives in Hertfordshire.

Pierce Brosnan

PETER CARRICK

ROBERT HALE · LONDON

© Peter Carrick 2000
First published in Great Britain 2000
Paperback edition 2002

ISBN 0 7090 7028 4

Robert Hale Limited
Clerkenwell House
Clerkenwell Green
London EC1R 0HT

A catalogue record for this book is available from the British Library

2 4 6 8 10 9 7 5 3 1

Set in 11/15½ pt Classical Garamond by
Derek Doyle & Associates, Liverpool.
Printed by
St Edmundsbury Press Ltd, Bury St Edmunds
and bound by
WBC Book Manufacturers Limited, Bridgend.

For Adam and Chloe Furr
Sam and Harry Bailey

Contents

Acknowledgements

Many people were of considerable help when I was researching and writing this biography of Pierce Brosnan. I am deeply indebted to each and every one of them, for their time, interest and cooperation, including those who wished to remain anonymous and are therefore not included here: Debbie Bailey, Frances-M Blake, Rita Boyce, John Cohen, Shirley Eaton, Sarah Furr, Brian Gayler, Roger Glanville, Barry Hobson, Owen Miles, Ron Millett, Christine Roberts, Michelle Roberts, John Walter Skinner, Dorothy Smith and Debbie Turner.

Many businesses, organizations and groups responded positively to my enquiries for information and I am exceedingly grateful to them all and to the people with whom I was in contact: British Broadcasting Corporation, British Film Institute, Elliott School, Hertfordshire County Council Library Service (Baldock and Letchworth Garden City branches), Millfield School, The Millfield Society, National Institute of Dramatic Art, Performing Arts Library, Hatfield, Herts, Theatre Royal, York, The Oval House Theatre, The Round House and UIP/MGM.

Other important sources of information were: *British Theatre Directory, Chambers Film and TV Handbook, Concise Oxford Companion to the Theatre, Daily Express, Daily Mail, Daily Telegraph, Empire Magazine, Evening Standard, Film Review, Flicks, Guinness TV Encyclopaedia, Kiss, Kiss, Bang! Bang!* (BT

9

Batsford) by Alan Barnes and Marcus Hearn, *Mail on Sunday*, *Night and Day*, *Pierce Brosnan* (Virgin Publishing) by York Membery, *Premiere*, *Radio Times*, *Sight and Sound*, *Sky TV Guide*, *Sunday Express Magazine*, *Sunday Telegraph Magazine*, *The Essential Bond* (Boxtree) by Lee Pfeiffer and Dave Worrall, *The Guardian*, *The Making of Tomorrow Never Dies* (Boxtree) by Garth Pearce, *The Observer*, *The Stage*, *Total Film*, *Wilderness Man* (Pocket Books) by Lovat Dickson, *You Magazine*.

List of Illustrations

Between pages 96 and 97

11

Illustration Credits

The Moviestore Collection: 1–14, 16–19, 23. Danjac, LLC and United Artists Corporation: 15, 20, 22. UIP (UK): 21. Owen Miles: 24.

Prologue

THE NEWS WAS SO BAD as to be almost inconceivable. It was like climbing Everest only to topple back just as you are about to gain the summit. Surely there must be some mistake. It was simply not possible that life could be so cruel, so devastating, so unfair.

From an early age Pierce Brosnan seemed destined to become James Bond, for the big-screen hero was to cut across his life at a number of crucial points in the years ahead. He would reveal that the first movie he ever saw that meant anything to him was the third 007 epic *Goldfinger* in 1964, when he was eleven. At the Odeon in London's Putney High Street, Sean Connery became an instant hero. Before that, back in remote County Meath in the Republic of Ireland, all Brosnan had seen were those flickering, ingenuous offerings of early Norman Wisdom and Old Mother Riley. He confided to a reporter some years later that he was blown away by *Goldfinger*. 'It was magic,' he enthused. 'I thought, I wish I was James Bond.'

He continued to follow closely the exploits of Ian Fleming's mythical hero through those boyhood days and well into adulthood. Then as a handsome 25-year-old struggling actor in London, he fell hopelessly in love with a beautiful blonde he met at a party, a meeting that would further his link with Bond. For the woman who would share his life as girlfriend and wife until her tragic, premature death was former model-turned-actress Cassandra

Harris. Shortly after that very first meeting she would step on to the film set of *For Your Eyes Only* in a fleeting role as Bond girl Countess Lisl von Schlaf. Brosnan accompanied her abroad on location shooting for the new picture and later they went together to the film's gala premiere in the West End of London.

Only a few years later Brosnan found himself recruited to take over as the new James Bond in succession to Roger Moore in *The Living Daylights*, released in 1987. The young actor was delighted that his links with Bond were to be forged in such a high-profile fashion. It was an enormous leap forward in his motion picture career. Amazingly he looked set to see his wild, romantic boyhood dream come true.

Until this time he had appeared in only a couple of largely insignificant big-screen movies released in 1980. The future seemed reasonably encouraging, but he was currently making faster progress on television, with minor roles in episodes of the long-running British series *The Professionals* and the *Hammer House of Horrors*. He would later boost his television reputation with *The Manions of America* and the BBC-made, nine-part series on the life of Nancy Astor, which would earn him a Golden Globe nomination.

This experience marked him out as a strong candidate when the producers of a new American-made spoof television series began their search for someone to take over the lead as the handsome, suave detective Remington Steele, in the show of the same name. At this point the most generous optimist would have been hard-pressed to predict the enormous success the new series would achieve. It was fortunate that Brosnan was in the United States at the time the series was being cast, hoping for a more significant breakthrough in his career. He had been unhappy with his progress in Britain.

Said Brosnan some time later: 'My agent in London had got me a list of introductions and we [Cassandra was with him] stayed with another agent in Los Angeles while I did the rounds. I had to move fast if I was to see everybody who mattered.' It was a hectic two weeks as he moved swiftly between agents and casting directors. It helped that *The Manions* had just been seen on television there, so when he heard that the title role for *Remington Steele* was still to be cast, he got in touch with the producers and secured himself an audition. 'They seemed to like me,' he explained at the time, 'but nothing happened.'

He held out little hope of success after taking the hint that he was not first choice for the part. Indeed he was already back in England when the surprise call came for him to return to Hollywood for a second audition. This time there were more influential people present to witness his performance, which he felt went reasonably well. Nonetheless he was surprised, largely because of his limited experience in big-screen movies, to receive news that the part was his. Disarmingly he suggested it was perhaps simply a case of being in the right place at the right time.

There was nothing particularly special or original about the Remington Steele idea, though the debonair character was, to a degree, cast in a similar mould to James Bond. Steele was to be a millionaire playboy-turned-detective, but at first the film-makers saw their hero as American, not British, and more mature, someone well into his forties. Brosnan fitted neither criterion. To Americans he had a noticeably British accent and was not yet in his thirties. No matter. He secured the part at just the right time, for Brosnan's diary was hardly congested.

Earlier, in Britain, he had completed his first film, playing a member of the IRA in the gangland thriller *The Long Good Friday* starring Bob Hoskins, but it was hardly an auspicious start. He was on screen for little more than a minute in just two fleeting appearances and did not have even one word to say. Nothing major seemed to be developing, and it was Cassie, perhaps more than Brosnan himself, who talked up the likelihood of better opportunities for him in the United States. The success of *Remington Steele* proved her right.

After a pilot of six episodes, the series began as a serious proposition in 1983. Starring Stephanie Zimbalist alongside Brosnan, it ran and ran, harnessing enormous popular appeal and impressive viewing figures. Soon it would be hard to locate a homestead in the United States which had not at some time watched or heard of *Remington Steele*. And Pierce Brosnan became as big a star and household name there as Larry 'JR' Hagman in *Dallas*. At its peak *Remington Steele* was screening twice a week. It was a punishing schedule. Brosnan found himself committed to an eighteen-hour working day. But the compensations were impressive. The show would become so popular that he was reported to be earning £20,000 a week, a phenomenal sum for a young actor at that time, and his fan mail topped fifty letters a day.

As the glossy Remington Steele, Brosnan became a television hero and heart-throb all over the United States. His following was immense. He achieved enormous exposure and recognition, at that time more than enough to deflect any possible ambitions he might have harboured about becoming James Bond. In any event Roger Moore, having taken over from Sean Connery some ten years before, had made himself such an automatic choice for 007 that there seemed little chance of the role becoming vacant.

Then the former television 'Saint' decided that playing 007 seven times in twelve years was more than enough. He was now fifty-seven years old, short of puff and visibly thickening round the waist. Though Moore was still young for his years, and fit, it came as no surprise when he decided to quit – and the urgent search was on for a replacement. Meanwhile, after achieving impressive year on year success, *Remington Steele* had begun to run out of steam. Ratings had fallen away badly. The decline was seen to be serious and NBC, the network that ran the series, decided to call it a day. The once 'essential viewing' television programme was abandoned.

16

For Brosnan the timing was perfect. He was now immediately tipped as the front-runner to take over as the new James Bond in the forthcoming blockbuster *The Living Daylights*, due for release in 1987. It was just what he wanted. His serious ambition was to be a major big-screen film actor, and you can't do much better than jump on the James 'Bondwagon' to get there. The idea of Remington Steele, with his handsome looks and cool persona, materializing as 007 captured the imagination of the public. It was an exciting prospect. The tall and handsome Brosnan looked every inch the natural successor to take over the mantle of cinema's great superhero. Newspapers and magazines responded with enthusiasm and were quick to speculate on the arrival of a new James Bond for the first time in fourteen years and seven Bond movies.

Almost over night the young Irish-born actor found himself the focus of enormous media attention. The mass-circulation media scrambled to tell his life story. The glossies tweaked out snippets for their gossip columns and enthusiastically splashed his handsome features on their covers. Brosnan, now dubbed 'the darkly handsome Irish actor in his thirties', had no trouble agreeing terms and went so far as to don Bond's trademark tuxedo for publicity pictures on the 007 soundstage at Britain's world-famous Pinewood film studios. He was on the verge of the biggest breakthrough of his career. To become a major star on the big screen, in what would probably rate as the highest profile role to be cast that year, was now within his grasp. He was all set to become the fifth James Bond in the most extravagant, outrageous and most successful big-screen movie dynasty in history.

Then came an outrageous irony. What Brosnan had not realized was that there existed a 'small print' clause in his contract with MTM, who had made *Remington Steele*, which gave them a limited time in which to secure a re-sale of the show. Meanwhile NBC, now fully alert to the sudden, enormous media hype and public interest in Brosnan and the new Bond movie – and on the back of some surprisingly good ratings achieved by televised re-runs of the series, seized the opportunity to reinvigorate their television character. A new deal was urgently struck between NBC and MTM on the very last day before Brosnan would have been free from his contractual commitments.

There was just no legal way out for Brosnan. On the brink of seeing his boyhood dream and greatest professional ambition realized, the opportunity suddenly spun hopelessly out of control. So a desperate, disappointed, and, for a time, angry 'James Bond who might have been' found himself securely tied to a new series of *Remington Steele*.

Years later when asked about missing out on Bond he shrugged his shoulders and said simply: 'Yes, I was disappointed at the time,' . . . and then, more trenchantly . . . 'pissed off in fact. I also felt a bit of a Charlie because every day there was some story about Bond and Brosnan in the press. But it was just business and I was caught in the middle.'

Once Brosnan became a non-starter, Timothy Dalton was drafted in to become the new James Bond in *The Living Daylights*, co-starring with Maryam d'Abo. The chances of Brosnan ever playing Bond now seemed remote, as Dalton continued in the high profile role two years later with the release of *Licence to Kill*. Brosnan, meanwhile, had returned to USA television in the role of Remington Steele. In total he would star in no fewer than ninety-one episodes, though the extension of the series was limited and not all that successful. By February 1987 the show had once again run its course. *Remington Steele* was soon nothing more than a pleasant memory for the millions of devoted American viewers it once attracted. Pierce Brosnan now felt certain that he had lost forever his chance to achieve his single most treasured ambition as a screen actor – to play James Bond in a blockbuster movie.

Or had he?

1
Tough Times

THERE ARE MANY BROSNANS throughout the Republic of Ireland, so when May Brosnan gave birth on Saturday, 16 May 1953, the safe arrival of the infant Pierce was hardly likely to stimulate widespread interest.

Tom Brosnan had been totally captivated when he first met May Smith at a local dance in Navan, the second largest town in County Meath, where May lived with her family. A handsome man, he had arrived in town from his birthplace of Tralee in search of work and had secured a good job with reasonable pay at a local furniture factory. May, who worked at a carpet factory in Navan, found Tom equally attractive and especially exciting, coming as he did from 'out of town'. They seemed meant for each other. They looked good together. She was pretty, he was handsome. Both came from traditional Catholic families. It soon became obvious that they were very much in love with each other. But as they made plans to be married, their ages alone threw some secret doubt on their long-term future happiness among well-intentioned family and friends.

Tom was almost thirty-seven years old. May had not yet reached twenty-one. Nonetheless, the ceremony went ahead as planned at St Mary's Catholic Church in Navan on Saturday, 16 August 1952, the very day many miles away that the Devon town of Lynmouth was devastated by floods that resulted in more than thirty deaths and thousands of people being made homeless. The unfolding story of the newlyweds would become sadly almost as torrid and turbulent as that dreadful Devon disaster; but at the time there was no sign of discord as the handsome couple happily honeymooned in Tralee.

Sadly, the physical attraction that had brought them together was soon less than enough to sustain the marriage. They found increasingly that they had little in common. Discord between them grew and arguments became more frequent. Tom was said to drink too much. Some would say that May, an attractive and active young lady, was far too young to be handling the day-to-day demands of a baby, which kept her at home when her more natural instincts drew her out. Tom, it was alleged, was unsympathetic and less domesticated than May had hoped. As the tensions grew May would find relief in spending more time with her parents in their home.

Both Tom and May soon realized that marriage had been a mistake and for a while remained together purely because it was in the best interests of baby Pierce. Few were surprised when, within two short years and after repeated rows and general discord, the marriage finally collapsed. May went back to live with her parents and Tom cut his ties with Navan. He left his wife and young son, going in search of work and a new life by moving to England.

Left alone in the small, close environment in which she had grown up, May Brosnan paid the price of her broken union. Her plight drew little sympathy from a strictly comformist community that, in the 1950s, scorned failed marriages as irresponsible. You were required to stay together whatever the differences, no matter how hard day-to-day life became. May was often cruelly blamed and humiliated – condemned as a single mother, even by some of her close friends. She became desperately miserable. Finally she found an escape hatch through her long-held ambition to be a nurse. She was a single-minded, determined young lady and her mind was made up. It was what she had always wanted to do and the present intolerable circumstances now provided the incentive. She managed to secure a trainee nursing post at a London hospital, and leaving her young son to be looked after by her parents, she too set out for what she hoped would be a better and more financially rewarding life in England.

Pierce Brosnan had been born at Lourdes Maternity Home in the town of Drogheda in County Louth, some fourteen miles south-west of Navan, and was named after three generations of Pierces running back from his paternal grandfather. He was still not old enough to attend school when, as years later he would explain with some contempt, 'I was abandoned by my parents.' Yet he quickly settled to life with May's mother and father, who gave him plenty of care, love and attention. They lived in a pleasant home, but sadly Pierce's young life was fated to be disrupted repeatedly over the coming years, as he was shunted from one family to another. He was only six when his maternal grandparents died within a few months of each other. The young boy was devastated, for, as he would later explain, he had loved them both dearly and they had looked after him well. Pierce's next home was with his Auntie Rosie, who soon found the strain of looking after him as well as her own family too much to manage. He then found himself living with 'Auntie Eileen' (his mother's great aunt, Eileen Reilly). The house was small, but the welcome was generous and loving. He felt settled and wanted in a young life that now carried an element of stability, perhaps for the first time.

Eileen's own son, though some years older than Pierce, became his first close friend. They shared a bedroom in the modest family home, and although there was little money within the household, Pierce was treated like one of the family. He would remain with Eileen Reilly for five contented years, and was considered by those

21

who knew him then to be a quiet, reserved lad, somewhat shy and not especially keen on physical activity or robust outdoor games. He was quite a homely young boy, though a weekly visit to the local cinema was the highlight of his life – that and the regular letters and pocket money he received from his mother, struggling to make a living and a new life for herself in London.

Youngsters are seldom diplomatic or sensitive. Reports from that time suggest that Pierce was sometimes branded by his young peers as an outsider, an orphan even, someone who was somehow different and, perhaps, not quite an equal because his mother and father had deserted him. Days at school would offer little salvation. Reasonably bright, if reserved, Pierce was reportedly bullied and bruised at his local Catholic school, which he attended from the age of eight. Discipline for all pupils was extreme, even by the standards of those times, and rigidly enforced. Transgressors were severely punished – the threat of a beating with a leather strap was never too far away.

Time passed, but it is difficult to know how Pierce saw his future developing, even if as a nine- and ten-year-old he thought about it at all. The trauma of being separated from his natural parents had diminished by this time, but he seemed to have little forgiveness in his heart, particularly for his father. Repeatedly in 'star' interviews, after taking Hollywood by storm, he would bring up how he was abandoned as a child and how he had seen his father only twice since the day he walked out on his wife and baby son. More charitable reports have suggested that Tom Brosnan, a carpenter by trade, originally left his family to go to England specifically in search of work. Certainly he would return to his roots from time to time, and a protective Eileen Reilly would be fearful of him getting too close to his son, particularly since she had not sought to become Pierce's legal guardian.

Time would appear to pass a harsher judgement on Tom Brosnan than on Pierce's mother May, though some reports suggested that he tried from time to time to contact his son and that he used to write to him and even send him money. Certainly his mother would keep in regular touch and send him money when she could hardly afford to do so, nursing and living in expensive London.

It was his mother who would bring about a significant change of direction in young Pierce's life. The time came when she wanted him to join her in London. It was a shattering turn of events for Auntie Eileen, who had long since come to regard him as one of her own family. She had always considered such a move a possibility, but had tended to push it to the back of her mind. But in truth she knew that for Pierce to be with his own mother was probably best for him. For by this time May was living in prosperous Putney, south-west London, in what was seen to be a stable relationship with her new boyfriend Bill Carmichael.

As he left the comparative obscurity of Navan for London's bustling metropolis the emotional farewells were quickly put aside. It was in Putney, settling into his new life, that he got to know his mother for the first time. She seemed strong-willed and positive after the relaxed and homely Auntie Eileen, but he settled well into his new surroundings and soon found his new 'stepfather' to be an easy-going, friendly person who welcomed his presence. And it was in Putney, of course, that the young Brosnan would see a James Bond movie for the first time. How he was impressed by *Goldfinger*.

It is hard to be certain whether Pierce himself realized at the time just what a difficult childhood he'd been forced to endure. Observers close to the family have suggested that it was overcoming these painful early years that led to his strength of character later in life. He would simply say years later: 'I made my way, by myself.' Then added: 'I didn't feel abandoned at the time. It was only later in life.'

Brief interludes and impromptu meetings would tend to focus

his mind, like the one and only time he met his father as an adult. Brosnan was over in Ireland filming the first episode of *The Manions of America* when a cousin fastened on to the idea of getting actor and father together. 'I didn't know what to expect, though I did wonder where he had been all those years when I most needed a father,' admitted Brosnan. They met at a Dublin hotel in 1986. Brosnan said: 'He was a stranger. I had not seen him for more than thirty years. Then there was a knock on the door and my father was standing there.' He told his son that it had never been his intention to abandon his family, but thought it best to leave while he searched for work. He was over seventy at this time and retired, but Brosnan said some years later that after talking about all kinds of things, they appeared to have little in common. By then he had come to regard his stepfather Bill as his real father. Of Tom Brosnan he said: 'He seemed like a nice man, but after waiting so long it was a disappointment . . . It was really all too late.' A few years earlier his comments had been a little more stinging: 'You'd say to yourself, "Tom Brosnan, why did you do it? Why did you leave?" ' By contrast Brosnan was more forgiving of his mother's shattering departure. 'It took courage to do what she did,' he reasoned. Even as recently as 1999, when being quizzed by a journalist about his parents, his responses indicated that the pain he felt from those early days had not been totally erased. 'Old Tom disappeared pretty quickly from my life . . . it was tough for me not having a father around,' he said. Then: 'But it was tougher for my mother. I admire her a lot.'

If years earlier, as he coped with the transition from small-town Ireland to London, he had perhaps hoped to be happier or make more of an impact at his new school, then he must have been disappointed with the Elliott Secondary School in Putney, which he attended for the first time on Tuesday, 8 September 1964, some four months after his eleventh birthday. In those days it was a mixed school with close to 1,500 pupils, many times bigger, noisier and more complex than his former school in Ireland. It is hardly surprising, then, that early reports suggest he was a quiet pupil, inhibited even, and well behaved both during and out of class; or that he failed to make much of an academic mark. 'I was always painfully shy and was easily embarrassed,' he would explain many years later. Simply changing schools was an enormous shock to his system. He had never before seen as many kids together in one place. 'I couldn't believe the size and I was so naive,' he remembered. Many of the pupils came from fairly poor backgrounds and lived on large council estates. The new Irish lad, along with youngsters from other ethnic-minority families, simply did not fit the mould and was an instant outsider to many of his fellow pupils. This often made him feel isolated.

His strong Irish accent set him off from the majority and identified him as a natural target for the school's bully boys. He was said to have been roughed up a number of times, but failed to respond to taunts and punches. They mockingly called him 'Irish'. When it came to looking after himself the young Brosnan, though much taller than most of his contemporaries, was something of a pacifist and would hesitate to defend himself. He was not 'physical' enough, and too much of a loner, for many of his classmates – and possibly for his own good. He did not join gangs or cliques and tended to keep himself to himself. He was already a nice-looking lad with a good mop of dark hair. More than anything at school he loved to draw. He seemed to have a natural artistic flair.

These were really formative years in an unfamiliar environment for a young Irish lad coming to grips with life in a big city. His comments some thirty years later seemed to hark back to those far-away schooldays in a London suburb. 'People have to find themselves,' he would say, 'just like I found myself.' Then he added, looking further ahead: 'I really found myself when I went to America as a young film actor,' the implication being that he still had some considerable way to go while he was struggling with the trauma of his new school in Putney. He was at Elliott School for almost five years, leaving there on Friday, 25 July 1969, a couple of months after his sixteenth birthday. Meanwhile, like most youngsters of that age, he had been spasmodically grappling with the future, without much success, and wondering how he might start earning a living.

Elliott School was founded as a comprehensive in 1956 and continues today to flourish under the guidance of head teacher Victor Burgess as a foundation school that achieved language college status in 1997. There seems to be little indication that Brosnan maintained any kind of links with his old school, but he might well be impressed by its present standing. Providing education for boys and girls (11–18 years), it emerged with distinction in the Office of Standards in Education Inspectors Report (1998) as an 'outstandingly well led and managed school' with 'examples of excellence at many levels'. The curriculum is wide and varied, and in the days when the young Pierce attended, Elliott School was perhaps ahead of its time in having a well-established drama section and its own theatre. While the current prospectus makes no mention of its now famous former pupil, Mr Burgess explained that the school has not only an excellent record of academic success . . . 'but also a strong tradition of cultural, artistic and sporting achievement'.

But it appears that the young Pierce was not particularly attracted to acting, and surprisingly, in view of his later ambition to become a professional actor, did not appear in any of the school plays. It was some time later that a tentative and somewhat nervous Pierce Brosnan chose to visit a nearby theatre organization called Group 64, where he was exposed to drama for the first time.

But it was while he was still attending Elliott School that we can glean the first, if hazy, vision of the future Pierce Brosnan, global superstar, with a powerful, magnetic attraction to millions of women worldwide. By this time Pierce had moved with his mother and stepfather to a new home in Fulham, and it appears to have been while out walking one day in 1968 on a nearby common that the loosely built, unsure and inexperienced fifteen-year-old gathered up his courage and secured a girlfriend for the first time. His now well-documented casual meeting with the pretty, dark-haired Carole Bevans, also fifteen and from Wallington in Surrey, was successful and significant. They were soon going steady and were to date seriously for almost two years before Carole called it a day. Many years later the young Pierce admitted that he had been devastated at the time by her decision to break off their relationship. But reports suggest that it did not take him long to recover.

For by then a vague idea that had been niggling at the back of his brain for a time was becoming increasingly important to him. Unusual for an uncertain teenager with such a turbulent domestic background, he began seriously to think about what he might do when schooldays came to an end. And in an astonishingly defining moment he wondered about the possibility of becoming an actor.

2
Life in Swinging London

As a teenager with no experience you don't simply leave school and jump straight into an acting job. It doesn't work like that. There is something called lack of experience that gets in the way. So at sixteen Pierce secured a job doing what he could do best: art and drawing. Straight out of school he became a trainee commercial artist with Ravenna Studios, which specialized as a photographic studio in premises just off Putney High Street. It was a convenient spot and not too far from the settled home life he was now enjoying with his mother and stepfather. He enjoyed working as an illustrator and the pay was in line with what an inexperienced youngster new to the work could expect. And most important, the employment was regular. Reports from those days suggest he was good at the job, dependable and conscientious. He said many years later: 'My interest in art was strong, but as time went on I felt I was being drawn more and more to acting.'

He was still passionate about movies and being in London in the latter part of the 1960s was just about the best place to be if you were a teenager. The city had been the swinging centre of the world for some years and in 1969 there was still plenty of Beatlemania around to deflect Pierce's attention from more serious issues.

But the young Brosnan had little concern for the antics of high-profile stars of the day, being more concerned with his own faltering steps as a trainee actor. He explained years later: 'Even then I wanted to learn all I could about acting and the theatre.' In reflective mood some twenty years on, he told *Film Review* that he had made his first public appearance in a production of *The Little Prince* at Southwark Cathedral in south-central London, just a short distance up-river from Shakespeare's Globe Theatre. 'It gave me my first taste for acting,' he said, adding that deep down he felt he had always wanted to act, perhaps at first just as a form of expression. In recalling those early days he would explain that he found 'sanctuary and salvation once acting came into my life. It was the best thing that ever happened to me.'

But it was his young work colleagues at Ravenna who pointed him in the right direction. Pierce explained: 'They knew my passion for movies and of my interest in acting, and it was through them that I was introduced to various workshop groups.' He would remain with Ravenna Studios for a couple of years while fostering a passion for drama, along with a growing determination and enthusiasm to learn as much as he could about acting.

He was seventeen when he went to a play at London's Royal Court Theatre in Sloane Square that had a profound effect on the course of his life. This historic theatre had opened in 1870 and specialized in innovative plays. The farces of Arthur Pinero were performed there in the 1890s, followed by premieres of some of the plays of George Bernard Shaw, whose bust would later stand prominently in the foyer of the theatre. The play witnessed by the young Brosnan was *Antigone*, a tragedy by Sophocles, written about 441 BC. In Greek legend Antigone is the daughter of Oedipus and Jocasta. When strife between her brothers, Eteocles and Polynices, results in the latter's death, she buries his body by night, against the order of King Creon. When her deed is discovered, the king condemns Antigone herself to be buried alive. She takes her own life before the sentence can be carried out, and Creon's son, Haemon, who was betrothed to her, kills himself over her body. The play starred the distinguished actor Stephen Rea, and it made such an impact on the impressionable Brosnan that he is said to have decided there and then that he must become an actor. It effectively changed his life.

He was not alone among actors in discovering that his quiet disposition, and inherent reserve and sometimes lonely nature could be transformed on stage as the occasion demanded. Nonetheless, it was a shock to the system when, urged by a friend at Ravenna Studios, he started attending the Oval House Theatre at Kennington Oval, close to the historic cricket ground. The Oval House was by no means a conventional theatre, but it provided the young and eager Pierce Brosnan with an informal, even casual atmosphere in which to overcome his initial fears and frustrations on stage. Situated in a multicultural area, the policy of the Oval House reflected the surroundings in which it was based. Even today it stages seasons of new work by radical companies, often dealing with issues related to women, lesbians and gays, blacks and Asians. While still supporting the development of work by new experimental professional artists, it presents a number of productions featuring workshop participants and Youth Theatre members. It was alongside kindred souls in an atmosphere of anonymity, excitement and adventure, that some thirty years ago the young Brosnan would increasingly lose himself. At the same time he found a settled and abiding home for his emerging ambitions.

What began tentatively would quickly develop; he was soon spending most of his evenings there. The acting workshops at the Oval House became central to his life and while the theatre's radical policy of concentrating on unusual and controversial presentations drew criticism from some conventional quarters, Brosnan looks back on those days as a vital period in his life. 'I was petrified,' he admitted years later when talking about his first visit to the Oval House Theatre Club. Hardly surprising, perhaps, considering he was the youngest member at the time.

Yet he said he somehow felt comfortable and 'at home' there. It was difficult not to loosen up in workshop sessions in which you stuck your tongue out at fellow students, screamed and raved with all the lunacy you could muster, and were instructed to touch and feel your fellow actors with sensitivity or intensity. Inevitably in such an environment personal inhibitions begin to wither, standing little chance of long-term survival against such brazen assault. And in the process you might well find that you were on the way to becoming a competent and convincing actor because of it. Many might have fallen by the wayside, but the Oval House has nurtured some rich talent over the years – though surely none richer in terms of international movie profile than Pierce Brosnan himself. But at the time he was not singled out as having any extraordinary potential.

What he did possess was a strongly focused will to become a good actor, and he threw himself energetically into his time at the Oval House, seizing every opportunity that came along. His confidence grew and so did his theatrical experience, in the rawest sense perhaps, as he joined fellow students in street theatre. In those days, unlike now, such activity was considered alarmingly eccentric by much of the general public. Many would simply gaze in disbelief at their antics. For Brosnan the Oval House was not just a place to go for an hour or two of casual diversion from routine. It quickly became central to his life. Even bedding down there overnight was not considered exceptional and in fact was often convenient. During the day he would act his parts with vigour and relish, cavorting and strutting with others on busy pavements and in well-known squares where people collected together. One time he performed as a clown, complete with floppy outfit, funny hat and red nose. Adding to the sense of camaraderie was a shared feeling that they were pioneering a brave, new kind of theatre, younger, freer and less structured than the mainstream equivalent. The Oval House was the ideal milieu for students with open, receptive minds and a desire to grow as much through self-will and experiment as through the conventional process of learning. And to show that he was up and among the best, he went through the ceremony of having his ear pierced at a ladies' hairdressers in Tottenham Court Road. Years later he revealed: 'I was eighteen, had my hair down my back and thought it would be cool.'

Oval House was known as a radical place when Brosnan arrived there in 1969, but it did, and indeed still does, possess two conventional performance areas where audiences of fifty (upstairs) and 100 (downstairs) can be accommodated. It was here, within a more disciplined structure and formal staging, that Brosnan extended his acting experience, appearing in a couple of productions in the upstairs hall. By now he was being picked out by some of his contemporaries for his serious passion for acting and the theatre. Fellow students from those days remember that his work had a real intensity about it.

Brosnan loved the time he spent at Oval House and it certainly did not undermine his ambition, but he knew he needed to move on. He was still only twenty when he enrolled for a three-year drama course at the Drama Centre in Camden, north London. It says much for his promise that he managed to secure a full grant on a course that was generally considered hard and where the standards were high. You didn't just walk into a place at the Drama Centre. There were always scores more hopefuls than could ever be taken on. Once inside, life was rigorous and disciplined. It was well respected as one of the very best places in town at which to learn your trade. Students had no easy ride there. The system expected high levels of discipline and dedication, which left little room for manoeuvre. Excuses were seldom tolerated and absenteeism, without a watertight excuse, was unacceptable.

Brosnan took it all in his stride, responding to the tough learning curve with exemplary determination. It was at the Drama Centre that he came down to earth and perhaps for the first time began to see life as it was likely to be as a professional actor – physically and mentally demanding, at times disappointing and demeaning and, yes, desperately risky.

But it was also at the Drama Centre that he exchanged the fantasy of himself as an actor for the reality of it all, when he played Oberon, king of the fairies, in the Centre's production of Shakespeare's *A Midsummer Night's Dream*. Three years is a long time and Brosnan was able to settle down at drama school, more than happy to let the grinding routine of learning his craft become a steady way of life. The days passed and his confidence grew. He seized every opportunity to widen his experience and extend himself as an actor, whatever the role might be, and was increasingly seen by staff and fellow students alike as a prepossessing figure with great potential. He was tall, looked good, moved competently about the stage and had an engaging voice that carried well and that by now was beginning to lose some of the more pronounced edges of his lilting Irish brogue. He was also highly self-disciplined.

He took whatever role came along, from Chekhov to light entertainment and now, by this stage, before a paying audience. He was being noted for the style and imagination of his performances and the fact that he often seemed to have a natural feel for a part. The drop-out level for potential actors is painfully high and even for those who do stay the course and are able to convert what was once a dedicated hobby or ambition into a paying career, the chances of becoming a top performer are remote. In the Drama Centre classes of 1973, '74 and '75, who could possibly have singled out Pierce Brosnan as a man to make it to the very top, to be a world superstar on the big screen? Surely, not even Brosnan himself.

In 1976 he took the chance to become assistant stage manager at the Theatre Royal in York at around £36 a week. While it might have fallen significantly short of his ultimate dream, it was still a job and it was in the theatre. That was important, and in the harsh light of day, more than he might have expected at the time. He was desperate for some realistic professional experience, and although the job of assistant stage manager is generally considered close to the bottom rung of the ladder in theatrical circles, it was coupled during his time at York with the opportunity to act as a legitimate member of the cast. These minor parts on stage did not compare with the more important, even leading roles he had carried off successfully at the Oval House, but nonetheless he relished these moments in a major provincial theatre, where he could perform in front of an authentic, paying audience. He even applied himself diligently, if with some surprise, when called upon to be a rustic farm-worker in a version of the great Harold Arlen–Yip Harburg stage musical, *The Wizard of Oz*.

His first appearance at York was as Sam Henderson in the Frederick Knott three-act thriller *Wait Until Dark*. The story is about a trio of con-men trying to outwit Susy Henderson, an attractive blind girl. Susy's photographer husband Sam is largely responsible for encouraging his wife to overcome her disability and was played, as a local press report suggested, 'with quiet confidence by Pierce Brosnan'. It was probably his first ever press notice. By way of explaining his somewhat meagre theatrical background, the official programme notes stated simply: 'trained, Drama Centre, London; first appearance in York; other theatres include Oval House Theatre Company.' But he did also receive a programme credit as the second of two assistant stage managers, listed below the stage manager and deputy stage manager. The show ran for a couple of weeks in August 1976.

Just three days later the then 23-year-old Brosnan was doing double duty – on stage as well as behind the scenes. As characters on stage, in order of appearance, he played Mike, second on stage, and then the first immigration officer (ninth on stage) in Arthur Miller's *A View from the Bridge*. In October that year (1976), for a three-week run, he appeared as a servant in Shakespeare's *Macbeth*.

Brosnan enjoyed his six-month contracted stay in York and by all accounts was generally popular with those he worked with, both on and off stage. He shared digs with a fellow cast member, absorbed the rough and tumble of life as a struggling actor-*cum*-assistant stage manager working in the provinces, and had to face the inevitable when his contract came to an end. What now? There was no work locally and he quickly returned to London.

The capital was equally barren. He wrote after jobs. He called on agents and theatres. He got in touch with anyone he thought might conjure up some work for him, however meagre or fleeting. No luck. He picked up any odd job that was going outside the theatre, to keep himself fed and his mind and body from seizing up. He had already considered knocking on the doors of art studios, where his natural talent would have kept him in food and pocket money. But that would probably have meant committing to a full-time job, leaving him little time to search and follow up any possible acting leads. He quickly abandoned the idea, since he never contemplated falling back on art and design as a substitute for acting.

The tide turned when he was cast in the Tennessee Williams play, *The Red Devil Battery Sign*, at the Round House in London's Camden Town. The venue was a disused locomotive shed, dating back to the mid nineteenth century. In 1961 it was taken over as a centre to make the arts more widely and easily available. This venture failed, but the theatre would later house some interesting productions 'in the round', including an experimental production of *The Tempest* in 1968 and later that year, *The Hero Rises Up*, a play about Nelson.

By May 1977, when Brosnan turned up for the first rehearsals of *The Red Devil Battery Sign*, the Round House had already become notorious. Always considered a natural venue for experimental theatre and unconventional productions of established plays, seven years before, amid enormous media and public outcry, the Round House had staged the previously banned new musical *Oh! Calcutta!* The show had actors and actresses cavorting naked on stage, and the show's creator, Kenneth Tynan, was attacked for 'tawdry, tasteless filth'. The police were in the audience for the first week, the Vatican said it was 'corruption on a grand scale' and the Dean of Westminster called it 'the prostitution of dramatic art'. But it ran for fifteen years and made a great deal of money.

Brosnan's break in *The Red Devil Battery Sign* seven years later was not destined to have such a long run, make as much money or create such scorching headlines, but it did turn out to be a significant signpost along his unfolding career path. Tennessee Williams's work is generally characterized by fluent dialogue and searching analysis of the psychological deficiencies of his characters. *The Red Devil Battery Sign* is not considered to be among his best, however, particularly when set against acclaimed blockbusters like *A Streetcar Named Desire*, *The Glass Menagerie* and *Cat on a Hot Tin Roof*. But Brosnan was happy enough to be cast, and even happier with his lot when he was unsuspectingly upgraded from his original role down the cast list to take over the part of McCabe, the young male love interest. It was a great opportunity and a good part for a young actor out to make his name.

Within two months the show achieved a stronger and more public profile when it transferred to the Phoenix Theatre in the heart of London's West End. This three-tier, 1,000-seater theatre located on the corner of Charing Cross Road and Phoenix Street, from which it takes its name, opened in 1930 with Noel Coward's *Private Lives*. But if optimism among the cast and crew of *The Red Devil Battery Sign* was high at the time of the move, then it was sadly misplaced. The show never made a profit and was soon building up worrying losses. The end was in sight within weeks, and once again Pierce Brosnan found himself on the theatrical scrapheap, searching for a job. Perhaps he could take a crumb of comfort from the fact that most critics appeared to blame the show's failure on its creator, rather than those who had done their best performing it.

3
Unsteady Steps on Stage

THE PREMATURE CLOSURE OF *The Red Devil Battery Sign* was a bitter blow for Pierce Brosnan. Having secured the part he had felt, perhaps for the first time since opting for a career in the topsy-turvy world of the theatre, that he could now relax a little and enjoy the benefits of a regular income, if only for a short time.

He would have been even more depressed had he been able to foresee the immediate future. Picking up work at that time in London's West End was virtually impossible. He was reduced to sending off dozens of application letters, getting in touch with contacts who might be able to help and generally chasing every remote possibility of work. Westcliffe-on-Sea, Essex, might not have been the centre of Brosnan's world at that time, but a positive response from the manager of the Palace Theatre there was something of a life-saver and applied a new gloss to the small seaside resort for the young actor. He was once again in the money, though only £50 a week.

As a career move Glasgow was seen as a step in the right direction when he secured a contract to appear at the Citizens' Theatre there in 1977. Indeed his time in Scotland would provide the opportunity to extend his experience significantly in increasingly important roles, first in Noel Coward's *Semi-Mode*, then *No*

Orchids for Miss Blandish, the well-known James Hadley Chase thriller, and later in a new adaptation of William Painter's significant work, *Palace of Pleasure*. Written in 1566–67 this work was largely composed of stories from Boccaccio, Bandello and Margaret of Navarre and was said to have become a major source for many dramatists, including Shakespeare.

But none of Brosnan's roles, however challenging, could claim to be uplifting. At Westcliffe, in *The Changing Room*, he had been a member of an all-male cast that seemed to be somewhat obsessed with nudity and rugged language. *No Orchids* brought in kidnapping and rape. And there was more than a passing reference to incest in *Palace of Pleasure*. Brosnan's naked appearance on stage at Westcliffe would have a television audience falling about when, more than twenty years later and now famous the world over as James Bond, he admitted to interviewer Des O'Connor the he had, sort of, stripped off. Off stage, however, Brosnan continued to be seen as a rather quiet and serious-minded individual, while at the same time building a reputation in the roles he played for strong focus, dedication and conviction.

It was these special professional qualities that enabled Brosnan to return to London for an important role in his second West End show. The flamboyant Italian film director Franco Zeffirelli's expansive talents would embrace such diversity as the staging of traditional grand opera at La Scala and the Old Vic to a lusty interpretation on film of *The Taming of the Shrew* with Elizabeth Taylor and Richard Burton and the casting of Australian action man Mel Gibson in a screen version of *Hamlet*. Zeffirelli had spotted Brosnan's potential in *The Red Devil Battery Sign* and later recalled how impressed he had been when he was preparing to stage the Italian play *Filumena* at the Lyric Theatre on London's Shaftesbury Avenue in late 1977. He cast Pierce in the role of Michele, the oldest of three brothers, one of whom, incidentally, was played by the later star of British television, Trevor Eve.

The show was well received by the critics, and the performance of Pierce Brosnan was singled out for particular merit. *Filumena* was also enjoyed by West End audiences and achieved a respectable run, enabling Brosnan to add convincingly to his developing reputation, if not greatly swell his bank balance. But the road ahead was still long and hard, and pitted with pot-holes to impede his progress.

In 1980 Brosnan returned to Westcliffe-on-Sea to star in the award-winning play *Whose Life Is It Anyway?*, and though the Essex resort hardly matched his ambitions, he was nonetheless encouraged to find that his reputation now meant that he could command double the wage he received there four years earlier. Soon he would be further heartened to discover that television producers were beginning to take an interest in him, though the big screen remained his ultimate objective.

His first fleeting appearance on the small screen came in an episode of the massively popular British secret-service series *The Professionals*, which ran on British commercial television for some six years from the late 1970s and made high-profile stars of its featured actors Lewis Collins and Martin Shaw. Brosnan was seen briefly as a wireless operator in an episode called *Blood Sports*, but was not required to utter a single word. He did better in an episode of the Hammer House of Horror called *The Carpathian Eagle*, with a walk-on part that allowed him to pick his way through all of a dozen lines of dialogue. But the money was useful and he was edging in the right direction.

The year 1980 turned out to be significant. It was then that the general public had the chance to see Pierce Brosnan for the very first time on a cinema screen, in the critically acclaimed British-made movie *The Long Good Friday*, directed by John Mackenzie. The earthy Bob Hoskins, who gave an outstanding performance as a doomed London mobster, and Helen Mirren were the stars of a film which was assessed by Halliwell as a 'heavily melodramatic

41

stylish updating of *Scarface* in a London East End setting.' As the embattled gangland boss in this compelling, violent drama, Hoskins was an undoubted star at the very beginning of his illustrious career. The picture also featured Dave King, Bryan Marshall, Eddie Constantine and Stephen Davis. Brosnan was way down the cast list and on screen for little more than a minute.

Yet for the would-be star, just being there on the big screen was a huge emotional and psychological boost; and 1980 would continue to provide optimistic and significant pointers to the future. He appeared in *The Mirror Crack'd*, a shallow Agatha Christie adaptation for the big screen that did little to impress anyone, either inside or outside the film industry, despite featuring a procession of top Hollywood stars of that time including Rock Hudson, Elizabeth Taylor, Kim Novak and Tony Curtis. It hardly set Brosnan's world on fire either. It brought just a single day's paid work, he did not move out of Britain, and had not even one word of dialogue to deliver. Only later was the choice of the experienced Guy Hamilton as director seen to connect in any way with Brosnan's future. The French-born Hamilton, distinguished for such films as *The Colditz Story* and later *Charley Moon* and *The Battle of Britain*, had by 1980 directed four of the eleven Bond movies so far released: *Goldfinger*, *Diamonds Are Forever*, *Live and Let Die* and *The Man with the Golden Gun*. He would not, however, direct any of the forthcoming Bond adventures which would feature Brosnan in the star role.

Remarkably, it was almost six long years before Brosnan would see the release of his next big-screen movie. Meanwhile he continued to build his reputation as a popular actor on television, making his small-screen debut in May of 1980 in a major role as Irish racehorse trainer Tyrone Donnelly in *Murphy's Stroke*, a dramatized documentary screened by the UK's independent television channel. Pierce was then cast in the principal role of Rory Manion in *The Manions of America*, a big-budget mini-series saga that was filmed in early 1981 at various locations in Ireland and the United States. Serious critics were quick to dismiss it, but the series made enough of an impact in America to bring Pierce Brosnan major recognition as a 'handsome hero' of the small screen and a new and exciting sex symbol.

Pierce later claimed that the remarkable level of response to his appearance in this series from American women viewers of almost all ages caught him completely unawares. His fan mail soared, and he later remarked that during the screening of *The Manions of America* he suddenly found women coming up to him in the street who simply wanted to touch him. He found it weird and scary.

His follow-up portrayal as the first husband of Nancy Astor in the successful £3 million, nine-part costume drama shown on BBC television sustained his popular appeal – a Golden Globe nomination added standing and prestige. Nancy Astor had died in 1964 after a significant political career in Britain. Though American-born – her maiden name was Langhorne – she was elected a British Member of Parliament in November 1919 in a by-election caused by the elevation of her second husband, Waldorf Astor, to the peerage. She was the first woman MP to sit in Britain's House of Commons and held her seat until 1945. During her political campaign Nancy Astor caught the imagination of the public as a vivacious and irreverent speaker. She said at the time that she intended to dress plainly, because 'I want to make it possible for the humblest woman who may be elected to follow the precedent I set.' In a colourful political life she championed the cause of women's rights and education and became known for her interest in social problems. She was a vehement temperance supporter and an ardent political hostess, and won a prominent place for herself in the House of Commons.

The series provided a good opportunity for Brosnan, and he was convincing as Nancy Astor's first husband, the Boston-born Robert Gould Shaw, whom she married in 1897 and divorced six years later. The marriage failed because of Shaw's heavy drinking and womanizing, and when the relationship turned physically abusive

Nancy Astor called it a day. It was not exactly the kind of role to bolster Pierce's candidacy as a 'leading man', but to his astonishment his growing number of female fans loved him just the same. Brosnan was required to age fifty years during the film, a remarkable transformation that was created by studio make-up expert Christopher ('Elephant Man') Tucker, though the dark moustache he wore for the role was his own.

By now Brosnan was on the brink of television big-time. *Remington Steele* was just around the corner and within months the first episode was screened by NBC in the United States in October 1982. There were no great expectations for the series at this point by anyone involved in the project and Brosnan did not expect to be in the United States for more than two or three weeks shooting the first few episodes, which could easily have been all that anyone might have seen of *Remington Steele*. Made by the established and highly regarded Mary Tyler Moore production company, which had already produced the enormously successful *Hill Street Blues* for television, studio executives began to pick up the first optimistic vibes at early private showings, but no one envisaged the long-running triumph the show would become.

The series quickly secured a loyal following for its pleasing blend of crime-solving adventure and light romantic comedy. It catapulted Pierce Brosnan to stardom. Brosnan delighted viewers with his consummate portrayal of the amateur detective, playing opposite Stephanie Zimbalist, daughter of Efrem Zimbalist Jnr, who had made his name in television in *The FBI* and *77 Sunset Strip*. He would appear as a guest star in one of the episodes.

The series, created by Michael Gleason and Robert Butler, concerns the ambitious Laura Holt, played by Stephanie Zimbalist, who opens a private detective agency under her own name, but finds it hard to generate business because not enough people have confidence in an investigations agency run by a woman. So ingeniously she creates an imaginary male boss for herself by renaming the business Remington Steele Investigations. This brings in the clients, but she soon runs out of excuses for the continuing absence of the 'top man'. She figures she must bring Remington Steele to life and conveniently the ideal candidate turns up on her doorstep in the handsome form of Pierce Brosnan, who, at the time, is more of a conman than a detective. But he is smooth, seems exactly right for the job and they get on well together from the start. So he takes on the identity of Remington Steele and joins the agency as a partner.

Viewers would be fed the occasional hint about a dubious past, but are offered little solid knowledge of Remington Steele (his real name was never revealed) and his background remains largely a mystery. But in addition to looking, speaking and acting the part impeccably, he also becomes a rather good detective. Clients love him. Business booms. One of his hallmarks, which the scripts exploited effectively, is the way he helps to solve cases by recreating memorable scenes from classic Hollywood movies like *Casablanca* and *The Third Man*. A further novelty, used now and then in series like *The Avengers, Batman, Man from Uncle* and *Girl from Uncle*, is that all the episodes of Remington Steele are named with some kind of 'Steele' pun in the title . . . *Thou Shalt Not Steele; Steele Crazy After All These Years; Signed, Steeled and Delivered* and *You're Steele the One for Me.*

The fact that an intimate relationship develops between Laura Holt and Remington Steele is not altogether surprising, but it is astutely handled by the background team. Viewers are treated to light flirtation in earlier episodes, but the affair fully blossoms only later in the series, becoming properly consummated in the very last season.

The series was slick and professional – all in all, excellent light entertainment. It was exactly right for its time. 'The romantic tension between the duo helped give the show some buzz and their sparkling repartee introduced a comic dimension to the plot, but it was never of the same level witnessed later in *Moonlighting* (created by one of *Remington Steele*'s producers, Glenn Gordon

45

Caron).' So wrote one industry critic, in a largely accurate assessment of the programme.

The series achieved impressive viewing figures in the United States and later in Britain when shown on BBC1 and then on Channel 4 between 1983 and 1987. The unexpected aspect of *Remington Steele* for Brosnan was that it propelled him to the top in the United States almost before he had secured a toe-hold in the UK. Very soon he was being hailed as the new Cary Grant, when he would rather have been identified as his own exciting self. But curiously, he was said to have modelled himself on Grant when later he pitched for the James Bond role after Timothy Dalton's unexpected departure, though Brosnan would wear an injured look when asked about it many times in the future. Years later he would repeatedly complain that throughout his career he was always being compared with someone. 'It was Cary Grant when I was doing Remington Steele, then Roger Moore when I signed to do James Bond; Steve McQueen much later when I did Thomas Crown . . . I could end my career as the new Mickey Rooney.'

The runaway success of *Remington Steele* astonished Brosnan. Despite continuing to seek recognition for his acting prowess, he did not exactly object to becoming a sex symbol. His ambition was strong and he certainly seemed to have no problems handling the dramatic switch from obscurity to major television stardom. He accepted the recognition as a prerequisite for the advancement of his acting career. What he liked less was the off-set tension that was said to exist at times between the two main stars. The coolness between them was said to be aggravated by the fact that Zimbalist, the more established star at the beginning of the series, was seen to have been eclipsed in popularity by her more callow co-star. But as Pierce might have pointed out at the time: that's show business.

4

Life with Cassie

WHILE PIERCE BROSNAN HAD BEEN finding his feet as an actor he had slipped out of adolescence into manhood. He was not alone among his generation in ditching convention. He would make up his own mind, do things his own way. He didn't appear to notice that he was behaving much the same as most young people of his age behaved. The important thing was to be noticeably different from people older than yourself, from those who had grown up before the teenage revolution of the sixties and seventies. This, combined with the coming of television and the mass media, gave young people, for the first time, an important and marketable place in a new and changing world.

If he was going to be an actor he needed to look the part. That meant dressing down in second-hand gear and dreary-looking extra-long top coats picked up from neighbourhood charity shops. He was still in his teens when he sampled his first cigarette. It was a badge of rebellion, along with wide flared trousers, long hair which covered his ears and, as an accessory to his occasional impromptu busking, a wig – or some silly fancy dress, in a contrived effort to get noticed. He would grow a moustache, then shave it off; cut his hair short, then let it grow long.

And he noticed that the world was filled with attractive-looking girls.

This was not a belated discovery. As he became older and more experienced in his relationships he would still look back with pleasure and a buoyant sense of awakening to the time when he and Carole Bevans, both just fifteen years old, had casually met and started going out together. As his first girlfriend, Carole would retain a unique place in his affections. When she dumped him two years later, unceremoniously during a phone conversation, he was shattered and moped about for days.

Meeting the Canadian Rebecca McKenzie while attending the Drama Centre in London restored his interest and confidence – and provided an altogether different experience. They met at a party, danced together and when Pierce asked her for a date she agreed. He took her on a day-long tour of London. Pierce said at the time that he wasn't interested in forming a long-term relationship. Acting was the serious thing in his life. He enjoyed female company, but he wasn't on the look-out for any kind of commitment. Even so their relationship became serious enough for them to move into a modest bedsit in Hampstead together.

Neither of them had much money at the time, and they lived a spartan existence to make sure they could make their weekly rent of £5. A close friend later revealed that they had bought each other wedding rings when they moved in, just in case the landlady objected to having an unmarried couple living in her house. They led a fun life together, in a relationship which seemed stable and enduring. Years later Rebecca said she looked back on those carefree days with joy, explaining that they were the best of mates, as well as early lovers.

They were together, living at two or three different addresses, for almost three years, but towards the end they simply began to outgrow each other. A visit Rebecca made to her parents in Canada enforced a short separation and when she returned the vital spark had gone. At first Rebecca tried to resurrect their relationship, but Pierce's lack of enthusiasm told its own story. His career was important to him and at the time he seemed reluctant to complicate his life with long-term commitment. A beautiful blonde named Cassandra Harris was to change all that.

Meanwhile Pierce led a far from hermit-like existence. He was attractive to women – tall, very handsome, if then a touch overweight, sympathetic, affectionate and amusing. While appearing on stage in Glasgow in 1978 he met Pattie Herley, a trainee nurse whose marriage had just ended, though she was not then divorced. Pattie responded enthusiastically to his advances and she described their relationship as 'loving and passionate' while it lasted.

It ended when Pierce returned to London after his stint in Glasgow. Later that year when he was twenty-five, he wrote to Pattie to tell her he had fallen seriously in love. Beautiful actress/model Cassandra Harris was the girl, and their meeting was destined to change the entire course of his life.

Cassandra was born Sandra Colleen Waites in December 1941 in Australia. She had early dreams of becoming an actress. In 1960 she enrolled at the National Institute of Dramatic Art (NIDA) in Sydney, an organization whose fine reputation made it a serious equivalent to Britain's RADA. (Mel Gibson, in the late 1970s, would acquire his early training at NIDA and, during one summer recess, make his first movie, *Summer City*, released in 1978.)

It was while attending NIDA that Cassie met Bill Firth, who would later become a highly successful businessman in Sydney. They married in 1964, but the prospects of a long-term liaison did not look good. Cassie continued to follow her ambition of becoming a successful actress and this meant spending much of her time away from Sydney, travelling huge distances from one major city to another doing the theatrical circuit in Australia. She and her husband seldom saw one another and divorce became inevitable, though they remained friends. Sandra's dedication to her career brought its just rewards, and bit parts in the theatre led to more important roles as she also began to win some encouraging exposure on Australian television. But in the late sixties Britain was definitely the place to be and she headed for swinging London town. Once in the capital she reinvented herself as Cassandra.

Her impact on London's smart scene was undeniable. She was a beautiful young lady, with natural blonde hair, an almost flawless face and an elegant figure; her cool, friendly personality made her an exciting person to be seen with. She was bright and outgoing, relished the social scene and was sought after at the swish 'in' parties of the day. It was at one of these smart social gatherings that she met Dermot Harris, younger brother of the more famous Richard Harris, the Irish-born film actor and one-time hell-raiser.

She and Dermot were soon living together in a fashionable home in Chelsea, but this new relationship was also ill-fated, though not before she had changed her name by deed poll to Harris and borne him a couple of children in less than a year. Charlotte arrived on Saturday, 27 November 1971 and Christopher on Saturday, 11 November 1972, both at a Wimbledon hospital.

Cassandra would never make the big-time as an actress, but she hit the headlines repeatedly, appearing in diary pages and gossip columns. She made an impact as a model, notably as the American Express girl in television commercials, and managed to sneak into a couple of films. But it was a well-publicised incident with singer Sammy Davis Jnr. which set the media ball rolling. As widely reported at the time, she was walking past the stage door of the London Palladium when Davis, who was starring at the famous London theatre, spotted her and asked if he could take her photograph. The picture saw the light of day in a glossy magazine and was evocatively captioned, ' "My Ideal Woman" by Sammy Davis Jnr.'

It didn't take long for the tabloids to latch on to the heaven-sent photo opportunities that Cassie's beauty and personality presented and she became a prized target. And Cassie didn't object, delighting in all the attention she aroused. But domestically things were turning sour. There had probably been squabbles with Harris before, but nothing as serious as the dispute that came after the children were born. Cassie said they ought to be married for the sake of the children, and according to her later statements, Dermot agreed. But nothing happened and although there was no official comment at the time, their relationship deteriorated. Their romance had always been turbulent, with rows between them commonplace, but for a time they appeared to settle down. There was even further talk of marriage, but it didn't happen. What did happen was that after being with Dermot Harris for almost eight years she suddenly walked out and never returned.

It was early 1979 and for the previous few months Cassandra had been seeing Pierce Brosnan. Once the curtains were opened on their affair, they both publicly expressed their love for each other. Much later, in March 1987, Pierce told *Film Review*: 'The best thing that ever happened to me was marrying my wife, Cassandra. We first met in Corfu, where she was making the Bond movie *For Your Eyes Only*.' In the fleeting role of the Countess Lisle, the expensive mistress of Colombo, played by Topol, Cassie proved her competence on the big screen. Agent 007, played by Roger Moore, spends a passionate evening with her, but she comes to a sticky end during an exciting chase sequence. It was generally accepted that she gave a sensitive and charming performance, albeit one that lasted only ten minutes. It was while they were in Corfu that Pierce was being considered for *The Manions of America* and he flew back to London to audition.

Brosnan was twenty-seven and Cassie thirty-nine when they married on Saturday, 27 December 1980 at the King's Road registry office in Chelsea, already famous for attracting society and top showbiz weddings. Cassie certainly wanted marriage, and

51

Pierce virtually insisted on it. He announced proudly that he did not want Cassie to be simply his girlfriend. His Catholic background played a part, but he also felt the need for closer ties with Cassie's children, Charlotte, then nine, and Christopher, eight. They would then be his legitimate stepchildren.

But the road ahead, unsure and unpredictable, was hardly likely to be paved with gold, not for the first few miles at any rate. Pierce was still a long way from making an impact in films, and on stage this was still a time when he regarded a return to Westcliffe-on-Sea as something of a triumph. But Cassie's fee from her Bond film helped see them into a house in Merton Park in London big enough for the whole family. Soon the main concern would be how best to capitalize on Pierce's growing experience as an actor in *Murphy's Stroke*, *The Manions of America* and *Nancy Astor*.

Cassie, far from being the archetypal dumb blonde, was shrewd, far-sighted and ambitious. Most of all, perhaps, she fully believed in Pierce's future, not simply as an actor, but as an important figure in the movies. While he was still a struggling actor it was Cassie who strongly fuelled his dreams of television and, in the longer term, film success. That is what he wanted, and she shared that ambition. Pierce would look back on those days, explaining: 'It was Cassie who believed in our move to America, even if we had to take out a second mortgage on the central heating to get there.' She recognized the move as a major step in his career, brushing aside all the doubts and inhibitions that instinctively made Pierce more hesitant.

In time Brosnan would probably have developed a career for himself in Britain; but he puts down the sheer speed of his success to moving to the United States. Cassie provided the resolve, courage and faith in his ability that enabled them to risk their last £2,000 to cross the Atlantic to Los Angeles and *Remington Steele*.

To his astonishment, the man who had always considered himself above all 'an actor' became 'a star' almost overnight. One heavy cloud would threaten their future, however. Not always in the best of health, it had been in early 1976, while living with Dermot Harris, that Cassie first experienced heart problems, undergoing surgery at London's world-famous Guy's Hospital. She left hospital, rested and recovered. The time ahead for both Cassie and Pierce was a wonderful adventure as he established his credentials as a movie actor. But sadly, Cassie's problem would not go away.

5

Big on the Small Screen,
but . . .

PIERCE BROSNAN WAS THIRTY YEARS OLD on 16 May 1983. He was eight months into *Remington Steele*, working long and committed days, and living with Cassie in a beautiful home in Los Angeles. He was thinking just how good life had turned out to be.

His prime aim, to break into big-screen movies, was yet to be achieved, despite those largely unnoticed glimpses in *The Long Good Friday* and *The Mirror Crack'd*. And now his aspirations were very much on hold, as the success of *Remington Steele* converted television work into a full-time job. At the series' peak he worked seven days a week for nine months. He said: 'We would complete ten pages of script a day and I was doing all my own stunts and fight scenes.' Not that he was complaining. Steele represented a major step up in his career and it was a well-paid job. The devastating, eleventh-hour collapse of his chance to take over as James Bond from Roger Moore was still two years into the future. Meanwhile he would cast a keen over-the-shoulder glance at Moore, the former highly successful television 'Saint', as he settled impressively into the 007 role in *Octopussy* (1983), and then *A View to a Kill*, released in 1985.

Years later Brosnan confessed that the runaway success of

Remington Steele gave him a fright. It came out of the blue and he felt totally unprepared for the instant recognition and exposure it brought. However, the demanding nature of the series did much to keep his feet on the ground. The workload was heavy and unremitting, but he found the part itself not all that arduous and he enjoyed the stability of being in regular employment for once. 'It was a light, sophisticated part with lots of charm,' he remembered. 'Luckily I had played a lot of similar parts in English stage comedies and was able to bring something of what they wanted to the character.' He told *Film Review*: 'As a bogus private eye I found there was room for wit opposite Stephanie Zimbalist as Laura Holt. Making the series provided my first experience of American light comedy.'

He was also glowing from the euphoria of Cassie's announcement in early 1983 that she was pregnant. Both had wanted a child together, and with the safe arrival of Sean William in September that year came a joyous fulfilment. Making *Remington Steele* became a routine, and the occasional journey for some special scenes was welcome, particularly a visit back home to Ireland for location shots for one episode. Another episode was shot in the summer in Britain, where the family enjoyed an enthusiastic welcome, since the series was currently being screened on UK television. A bonus about *Remington Steele* for Cassie was that she was able to make a few guest appearances as an earlier mistress of Steele; another episode even featured Charlotte and Christopher.

Despite the enormous success of the series Pierce and Cassie continued to be fiercely ambitious. Both had their eyes firmly focused on the big screen for Pierce's long-term future, and when Cubby Broccoli offered him the part of James Bond in the summer of 1986 their ambitions seemed to be well on track. As the picture was to be shot in Britain, Pierce and Cassie hurriedly made plans to return to London. When everything fell apart in that most dramatic and agonizing fashion – and Pierce lost his chance to be James Bond, seemingly for ever – their future was torn apart.

But away from filming there were disappointments too. He and Cassie talked about having another child quite soon, while Cassie felt young enough; but it didn't happen, perhaps because her age might already have been a problem. They considered adoption, but never went ahead with it. Aside from family matters Cassie sometimes felt she might like to do a little more serious acting – nothing really grand or ambitious, but not just cameos or guest spots. Again it never amounted to anything. Nor did their desire to act together in some project, in television or movies. And disappointingly, in view of their clear, combined objective for Pierce to move into big-screen movie-making, he was to exchange one television treadmill for another as *Remington Steele* came to an end. As ever, chance, fate and timing seemed to be dictating events.

Not long after the final episode of *Remington Steele* Pierce took the central role in a new eight-hour television mini-series called *Noble House*, screened in 1988. It featured, among others, Scottish actor Gordon Jackson, a household name in Britain after his role as the butler Hudson in the television series *Upstairs, Downstairs*.

About a year later, despite Pierce's declaration that *Noble House* would be his last television mini-series for a while, he contradicted himself by taking the role of the redoubtable Phileas Fogg in a small-screen version of Jules Verne's classic tale, *Around the World in Eighty Days*. Back in 1956 American showman Mike Todd, one-time husband of Elizabeth Taylor, had realized a long-cherished ambition by bringing the story to the big screen just prior to his death in an air crash in New Mexico. David Niven had the starring role in Todd's original, with Robert Newton cast as the detective Mr Fix. A host of other familiar celebrities to appear included Shirley MacLaine, Charles Boyer, Joe E. Brown, Hermione Gingold, Trevor Howard, John Mills and even George Raft and Frank Sinatra. As Halliwell concluded: 'What was breathtaking at the time seems generally slow and blunted in retrospect, but the fascination of recognising forty-four cameo stars remains.' None the less, it won an Oscar and was, in the mid 1970s, one of the top box-office hits of all time.

There were fewer cameo appearances in the Brosnan small-screen version, but among the established stars readily spotted were Patrick MacNee, of *Avengers* fame, Lee Remick, Robert Morley, Jill St John and Jack Klugman, the famous detective in television's *Quincy* series. Jules Verne's famous nineteenth-century story sees socially correct, upright English aristocrat Phileas Fogg playing cards in his London club. There and then he accepts a gentleman's wager that he can travel round the world in eighty days. The film follows his many, varied and wondrous adventures in the completion of his task, which include flying in a balloon, being involved in a shipwreck, being accosted by an aged prostitute in France and fighting off an attack by American Indians. Despite overcoming all these and other desperate experiences Phileas lives to tell the tale and win his wager. Peter Ustinov was cast as Detective Fix in the role occupied by Robert Newton in the earlier, big-screen interpretation.

The critics were not sufficiently impressed to mark the mini-series for posterity, but it certainly hit the jackpot for entertainment value and widespread appeal, and captured the attention of the viewing public.

Around this time and into the early 1990s a number of television producers targeted Brosnan, and he began to appear in several romantic dramas, thrillers and light comedies. Appearances in programmes like *The Heist* and *Victim of Love* were never intended to stimulate the intellectual nether regions of the most serious critics, but they did provide entertaining viewing for large swathes of women across the United States, who fell for the handsome looks, restrained presence and the exciting physical persona of Pierce Brosnan.

Noble House was different. Costing some $10 million to produce, this mammoth television mini-series was made by famous Italian film director Dino De Laurentiis. He made his name by producing some prestigious Italian films with the legendary Carlo Ponti in the 1950s – but his taste for grandiose overblown international productions would lead to some expensive failures in the late 1970s and early eighties. *Noble House* was based on James Clavell's best-selling story, set in the sixties, of a shipping firm's fight for existence, set against the wheeling and dealing of a Hong Kong trading house.

Brosnan seized the opportunity to do *Noble House. Remington Steele* was over and the chance to play James Bond had been kicked from under him. He accepted this new assignment gratefully and as some consolation for his flagging spirits, particularly as there appeared to be little else on offer. He got the feel of his role as Ian Struan Dunross, head of the powerful Noble House company, by doing on-the-spot research in Hong Kong.

The plot centres on deep intrigues and conspiracies, with Brosnan's love interest provided by the 35-year-old Deborah Raffin, all set against the tense, sweltering background of Hong Kong. 'I had nothing much else to do at the time,' commented Brosnan pointedly some time afterwards. He also conceded that his co-star was possibly a trifle old for the part of his lover and that the film was somewhat sombre and too full of anxiety and brooding. He told a reporter: 'Having done it, I realized I'd rather play characters with a little more humanity and vulnerability.' It was a big and demanding part, since Brosnan was featured in almost every scene, and overall *Noble House* did no harm at all to Brosnan's credentials as an actor of some depth and versatility.

His ambition to become a serious, creative actor, however, was already being somewhat thwarted by his being pigeonholed as an archetypal leading man. His 6' 1" height, cool bearing and measured voice, which still carried a trace of the lilting Irish about it – all were factors. Surely, it could only be a matter of time before the movie world's big guns saw the enormous potential in the man.

You might claim, optimistically, that his big-screen potential had already been spotted when he was singled out by director John McTiernan to play a starring role in *Nomads*, released in 1986. McTiernan, a former writer and director of television commercials, would soon build a well-earned reputation as a big-movie director with *Predator* in 1987, *Die Hard* in 1988, one of that summer's more entertaining blockbusters, and *The Hunt for Red October* in 1990 starring Sean Connery. This latter picture gained the vote of the American entertainment paper *Variety* as 'a terrific adventure yarn excitingly filmed'. The director's treatment of the Tom Clancy best-seller, steering his way cleverly through an involved plot, was said to prove beyond doubt his ability to handle the complicated mechanics of film suspense.

In those earlier years Brosnan was proud to be working with McTiernan, who had been born into a world of entertainment, his father being an opera singer. He had worked backstage, at the same time handling bit parts, in his father's productions long before reaching his teens. Later he designed, directed and acted in summer stock and regional theatres, before graduating from New York University to become designer and technical director at the Manhattan School of Music. McTiernan would make some 200 television commercials but, like Brosnan, he was deeply ambitious to make his mark in film-making. Pierce could not have wished for a more appropriate choice as director for the first movie in which he had a starring role, because, in the space of just four films, McTiernan would establish himself as one of Hollywood's most gifted and profitable directors of suspense.

Indeed, Brosnan and McTiernan were both breaking new ground with *Nomads*. It was the director's first feature film, which he had also written. It was an involved, off-beat story about a French anthropologist (played by Brosnan) in Los Angeles who becomes involved with a band of scary street people. It was a fantasy-*cum*-horror story starring London-born Lesley-Anne Down, who, aged thirty, had already appeared in more than a dozen movies. Working with the suave Remington Steele (Brosnan would make the film during a break in shooting on the series), would hold no fears for the beautiful and experienced actress, who had already co-starred with such Hollywood heroes as Harrison Ford, Burt Reynolds and John Wayne. In Britain she was probably best remembered for her portrayal of the aristocratic daughter in the long-running television series, *Upstairs, Downstairs*.

Nomads had her involved with a very different Pierce Brosnan from the smooth, elegantly dressed and impeccably mannered Remington Steele. The plot evolves through a series of flashbacks, but the opening scene, as early publicity hinted, has Brosnan lying on his deathbed in hospital, dirty, bearded, bloodied, yelling crazily and punching Lesley-Anne Down to the floor before ultimate darkness overtakes him. Former pop group member Adam Ant was cast as the villain of the piece.

Nomads was a low-budget movie with little apparent intention to turn the world upside down, though reviews were mixed and probably better than expected for such a narrowly focused movie. Pierce later commented on his dramatic change of image for the picture. 'I maybe went too far with a beard and growing my hair long for *Nomads*; it may have been a mistake as the picture didn't do very well.' Meaning, perhaps, that such a total change of image might have put off his *Remington Steele* faithfuls to such an extent that they simply gave the picture a miss.

He had no such problems with his next film. Any hopes that *Nomads* might be his big breakthrough looked like being confirmed when he was offered an important role in *The Fourth Protocol*, which would go out on general release in the year after *Nomads*. The new movie was littered with star names. He would be working alongside Michael Caine, whose superstar pedigree extended back to the sixties in such popular classics as *Zulu*, *The Ipcress File*, *Alfie*, *The Italian Job* and *The Battle of Britain*; and right through the seventies with *The Eagle Has Landed*, *A Bridge Too Far* and *The Poseidon Adventure*. More recently there had been *Educating Rita*, with Julie Walters, and *The Honorary Consul* (*Beyond the Limit*, in the US), in which he starred with Richard Gere and Bob Hoskins.

The film, shot in the spring and summer of 1986, was directed by the illustrious British-born John MacKenzie. He had already won critical acclaim for his seminal *The Long Good Friday*, the London gangland movie of 1979, which featured fine performances by Bob Hoskins, Helen Mirren, and in which, of course, Brosnan had made his big-screen debut. Frederick Forsyth, on whose best-selling book the new film was based, also served as an executive producer of the picture, alongside Michael Caine and Wafic Said. It was very much a British effort and Brosnan welcomed the opportunity to return to England, where a good deal of the shooting took place in and around Milton Keynes, Chelmsford, Ipswich and Colchester. As a spy thriller that pitted East against West, the forces of democracy against the power of Communism, it is perhaps not altogether surprising that the less suburban scenery of Rovaniemi, Finland in the Arctic Circle, was chosen for the scenes supposedly set in Russia. To be sure, the location was a good omen, for it was there that Caine had shot many of the scenes for his enormously successful *The Eagle Has Landed* ten years earlier. Michael Caine, as British spycatcher John Preston, is the lead in *The Fourth Protocol* in a role not dissimilar from the character of Harry Palmer in the film that made him an international star, *The Ipcress File* – sardonic, cynical, the man with a mission who is not above bending the rules if the occasion demands. Brosnan plays the bad guy, Major Petrovsky, whose purpose in life is to assemble an atomic bomb at an American air base in Britain, the objective being to force that country to remove all its US air bases. But in doing so Russia would be breaking the secret fourth protocol to the 1968 Nuclear Non-Proliferation Treaty.

Frederick Forsyth wrote the screenplay, while additional material was provided by Richard Burridge. Good on-screen support was provided by Ian Richardson as the smooth, yet devious Sir Nigel Irvine of the British secret service, and Ray McAnally was a convincing General Karpov, head of the KGB. Brosnan looks more groomed than in *Nomads*, but not yet back to his dapper Remington Steele, wearing longer hair and a growth of bristles that almost masquerades as moustache and beard. Anton Rodgers was also included in an impressive cast. Joanna Cassidy provides Brosnan's love interest, and in a publicity still that shows both of them naked between the sheets Brosnan is aiming a gun through the pillow at Cassidy's chest. The clever caption suggests that Pierce '. . . brings a new meaning to pillow talk'.

Alan Frank, writing in *Film Review*, found *The Fourth Protocol* 'thrilling, suspenseful and very entertaining'. The same writer considered that Brosnan had done well on being released from the formulaic straitjacket of Remington Steele. Added Frank: 'He effectively conveys the ruthlessness of the character as well as his surface likeability and, while his part offers him no major dramatic challenges, Brosnan makes it credible and is a worthy opponent for Caine.' Terence Doyle in his more critical review in *Film and Filming* aimed at the heart with: 'Forsyth's vaunted reputation for convincing detail takes a blow as all we learn about Russians is they drive black cars at a snail's pace and shake their heads in confusion a lot.' Then he turns his sights on the Russians' crack agent: 'Petrovsky (Pierce Brosnan) gets to ride a motorcycle whilst in England (trying to get his bomb into a US air base), but he never gets a chance to show off his splendid command of English. He just shakes his head some more.'

Brosnan did not see it quite like that. 'There's a lot of suspense in the film and *The Fourth Protocol* is going to have audiences sitting right on the edge of their seats, I promise you,' claimed the enthusiastic star. The opportunity had come at a good time for Brosnan. He said he had been living on a knife-edge between *Manions* and *Steele*, and an important movie like *The Fourth Protocol* was something he had been hoping for. 'I jumped at the chance,' he said.

It was certainly something of a boon to be working on a mainstream movie with someone of the standing of Michael Caine. But despite the optimism, the literary authority of Forsyth, and Caine's pulling power, *The Fourth Protocol* did not make much impact on the paying public.

Brosnan's enthusiasm for making movies was obvious from the comments he made when working on *The Fourth Protocol*. 'I love everything about movies,' he said. 'Although I was trained for the stage and got my first real break on TV, it has always been my ambition to have a good role in a really big movie like this one.' During a break in filming at Elstree Studios, where the picture was being shot, he added: 'This is the best role I've had yet on the big screen. Also it makes quite a change to be playing a villain after so many clean-cut heroic characters. For me, this part in *The Fourth Protocol* has been well worth waiting for.'

He consolidated his movie credentials with featured roles in two more films released the next year, 1988. He was cast in the lead role in *The Deceivers*, an Anglo–Indian production directed by Nicholas Meyer. Written by Michael Hirst from a novel by John Masters, it follows the exploits of an English army officer serving in India in the 1820s who infiltrates a sect of murderers that have formed themselves into a secret society.

Brosnan spent two months in India making the film, and he certainly looked the part in his scarlet jacket and white trousers, along with thick hair and bushy side-whiskers. Much of the shooting took place in and around Jaipur, a beautiful oasis town, which, along with New Delhi and Agra, now forms what is known as the Golden Triangle, a much prized tourist route. Jaipur, also known as the Pink City because of its many fine buildings built in pink sandstone, is one of India's loveliest cities. It is also famous for its enamel work and jewellery.

Actor Saeed Jaffrey, who ten years later would play the corner-shop owner in *Coronation Street*, also starred in *The Deceivers*. The film did not impress the critics, however, and failed to excite the punters, but for Brosnan it represented just one more step back from television, and a half-step nearer his big-screen ambition.

It could hardly be claimed at this point that Brosnan was setting the film world alight. As he toiled away on productions that relatively few filmgoers wanted to see, it must have been a bitter experience to witness the worldwide hype being lavished on the next James Bond movie. Timothy Dalton, born in Colwyn Bay in 1944 – and therefore some nine years older than Brosnan, though seventeen years younger than Roger Moore – had attended RADA. On stage he had proved his versatility in a number of plays and particularly on film in two contrasting roles, as a model of effete venom in the 1968 *The Lion in Winter* and as a sensual, charged Heathcliff in the 1970 *Wuthering Heights*.

Cubby Broccoli had picked out Dalton as a possible James Bond when Roger was originally cast for *Live and Let Die*, released in 1973, and was delighted when he accepted his invitation to take over the role from Roger Moore. His substitution for Brosnan was confirmed on 6 August 1986, and filming began at Pinewood about eight weeks later. Dalton's casting was seen by a number of insiders as a sound move strategically, for the Welshman was considered to be fully capable of bringing a more contemporary, cynical edge to the Bond character. Broccoli felt it was important that his hero should keep in step with the times.

Meanwhile, Brosnan concentrated on his own career, which continued to sputter along in fairly inconsequential fashion. *Taffin*, made before *The Deceivers* but released in the same year (1988), again failed to excite cinema audiences. Shot largely on location in Ireland, it tells the story of Mark Taffin (Brosnan), a handsome, devil-may-care debt-collector who becomes involved in a big-business conspiracy. A one-time candidate for the priesthood, Taffin is an enigma, a loner who turns into a reluctant hero when fellow residents recruit him to stop unscrupulous businessmen from constructing a dangerous chemical plant in their small, picturesque town.

The thriller, which also featured Alison Doody as Brosnan's co-star and Ray McAnally from *The Fourth Protocol*, was directed by Francis Megahy. The Irish-born McAnally, widely regarded by insiders as a fine actor, would later have his talents more publicly acknowledged – namely, the 'best supporting actor' accolade for his performance in the movie, *My Left Foot*, starring Daniel Day Lewis, in 1989, the year in which McAnally sadly died, on 15 July.

The chance to work in Ireland again, and the intriguing nature of his role, both had bearings on Brosnan's decision to accept. Indeed he was pleased with the outcome. 'As the ideas progressed, a western theme gradually developed and I incorporated it into *Taffin*,' he explained. 'I wanted the character to wear dark colours and we added the leather jacket and cowboy boots to complete the image.' He was also intrigued by the way Taffin, as he explained, '. . . uses violence in a very cerebral way, believing that the threat is far more terrifying than the actual act.'

But once again, *Taffin* was hardly the success everyone involved had hoped for, critically or commercially. This was particularly disappointing for Brosnan, who, in this film and *The Deceivers*, could hardly claim to have made an altogether auspicious start in his bid for stardom

Yet all that would soon be the least of his worries.

6

Desperate Days

CASSIE HAD NOT BEEN in the best of health for some time, but the official diagnosis in December 1987 that she was suffering from ovarian cancer came as a devastating blow.

Though by no means a top Hollywood player, Brosnan nonetheless had been well paid for his work on *Remington Steele* (the final episode had been broadcast just ten months before, in February 1987). Other television and film projects had also brought in good money, so that the family now enjoyed a comfortable, indeed luxurious lifestyle.

They lived in an attractive seven-bedroom house, situated in a desirable area of Los Angeles. The family was close and loving, the husband and wife never more happy and contented than when they could spend time together. The trappings of the good life were all there to be enjoyed, but the Brosnans were never an integral part of Hollywood's party-going set.

The world's press had gone mad when Pierce and Cassie first got together. Individually they were a strong attraction for photographers and columnists. Together they became a truly 'cool couple' and their media focus soared. But privately they were happy to escape the spotlight, their joy from simply being together or with

67

close friends transcending all the glitz and glitter of Hollywood.

Relaxing in the comfort and privacy of their home allowed them treasured moments in a busy life, and when filming took Pierce away, Cassie would sometimes accompany him on location. Only nine months before Cassie received the dreadful news, a happy and contented Pierce had told a reporter: 'I know I've been very lucky. I have a nice home with Cassie and the kids. My career is going well and I can't complain.'

Some twelve years later the memories still lingered. In an interview with *You* magazine in 1999 he told reporter Gabrielle Donnelly: 'I was very happily married for seventeen years, but when I was first with my late wife nobody knew who I was, so it was simple. I owe my career to her because she encouraged me to take risks. If she'd listened to me I'd still be living in a little flat on the King's Road, worrying how I was going to pay the milkman.' In fact they had been together for seventeen years, married for eleven. Together with the now teenaged Charlotte and Christopher, and four-year-old Sean, the Brosnans were considered a glowing example among the superficiality and shifting allegiances that characterized much of Hollywood life.

Cassie shared Pierce's views about bringing up the children. They wanted the best for them, not just in educational opportunities and financial security, but also in terms of a loving and stable family life. When the time was right, and to protect them from the worst excesses of an indulgent Hollywood lifestyle, Charlotte and Christopher went to Britain to continue their education at one of the country's top private schools.

Millfield School, in an area of Somerset with historical links to the legendary King Arthur, was founded in 1935 with the specific aim of getting its first seven boys, six of them Indian princes, into British universities and of expanding in due course to twelve pupils. This objective was quickly achieved, on the back of a declared policy of high-quality teaching leading to excellent examination results within a family, country-house atmosphere.

The school specialized in providing a sound education in all subjects, and students were encouraged to take a full and active part in school life. At first only boys were accepted. The school technically became co-educational in 1938, when just one girl joined. It was not until midway through the Second World War that there were sufficient girls at Millfield for them to share places evenly in a mixed bicycle polo team! The school attracted many youngsters whose parents were rich or famous in some way. So Charlotte Emily and Christopher Ivan Brosnan could not expect, nor indeed were given, any special treatment. Pierce and Cassie saw it as a way of keeping them level-headed, with their feet firmly on the ground, as well as providing them with a thorough education. Both children joined Millfield in 1986. Charlotte, almost a year older than her brother, joined the third year A stream group, the younger Christopher being placed in the second year A stream group. Barry Hobson of the Millfield Society explained that all pupils are asked to aim for excellence in their activities. He added: 'Most of them would stress the homely atmosphere in the houses and the degree of "freedom" which could be earned. Perhaps this is what makes Millfield different.' By 1970 the pupil numbers had risen to almost 1,000, with 150 tutors. For the last fifteen years pupil numbers have been restricted to a top level of 1,500. Charlotte and Christopher spent four years at Millfield, both leaving in 1990.

Today Millfield amenities are considered to be better than those of many British universities, let alone boarding schools. Set in sixty-seven green and woody acres in the middle of picturesque Somerset, the school has eighteen tennis courts, two nine-hole golf courses, a theatre and an Olympic-size swimming pool. Pierce felt it important that at least some of their education should be in Britain, to give them a sense of, and feeling for, their family roots. Meanwhile, closer to hand, young Sean continued to be a joyful reminder of the happiness that Pierce and Cassie had found together.

There was a history of cancer in Cassie's family and the fear of its being passed down cast a heavy shadow that never completely faded away, even in her most positive and healthy times. More recently she had been excessively tired and listless. Cancer has been dubbed the silent killer because by the time the symptoms become visible, the disease has usually spread too far. When her stomach became swollen, Cassie naturally was worried and suspicious.

There had been a profound sense of relief, all so recently it seemed, when Cassie had been told by a specialist in California that she was in good health and there was nothing to worry about. All the more cruel and traumatic, then, was the verdict of a second gynaecologist just a few months later that there was, indeed, a good deal to worry about. The shock was immense. Cassie and young son Sean had been enjoying some time away in India, where Pierce was doing location work for *The Deceivers*, which was made during the autumn/winter of 1987. It was on their arrival in London, en route to their home in Los Angeles, that Cassie had gone into the Portland Clinic for tests.

The prognosis was grim. It was left to Pierce to break the news of their mother's illness to Charlotte and Christopher when he greeted and comforted them on their arrival in London from school in Somerset. They went immediately to Cassie's bedside. They were frightened and distraught; it was Pierce who would provide the strength, support and, indeed, hope during the difficult days ahead. The malignancy was well advanced and the expressed medical opinion worryingly non-committal.

Pierce cleared his diary, cancelled all his professional commitments, and against Cassie's assurances that she would be all right in London continuing her treatment while he went back to work in the United States, he stayed close to her, helping her fight the trauma which had struck with such speed and punishing impact. The family were in deep shock. Cassie's treatment was unpleasant and in itself debilitating, but essential if she was to stand any chance of improvement or recovery. The older children, now sixteen and fifteen, were a wonderful comfort to them both while the four-year-old Sean seemed anxious to do what he could to help, without knowing too much of what was going on.

Pierce would explain later with obvious pride that Cassie had shown 'great dignity, courage and humour' when confronted by her illness. If anything, this deeply troubled time drew the family even closer together; it was a togetherness that gave them all the fortitude, hope and will to carry on. Pierce and Cassie had rented an apartment in London, and as Christmas approached, they decided to celebrate in the usual way. The place was decorated with a tree and bunting and, as Cassie announced later in glowing terms: 'My husband even cooked Christmas Day lunch himself.'

She revealed with great affection and pride how they all worked together in practical terms to help her maintain the strict regime necessary to fight her illness: 'My husband and children all went on my diet to help me stick to it. It was their way of showing me how much they supported me.' She seemed to find an inner strength in dealing with her illness by getting to know as much as possible about it, in almost a detached way, though days were seldom comfortable. She would quiz the doctors about the treatment she was being given; even challenge them now and then. Naturally she wanted to be told about all possible benefits. She read as much as possible about cancer and up-to-date treatments and talked openly about her illness. Her interest was almost scholarly, as if she might be preparing for an examination in the subject. In some curious way this approach seemed to give her courage and helped to divert her mind from the debilitating, personal aspects of her illness. She also took to meditation and tried out other regimes that she felt might help, like special diets.

Surgery was inevitable, as were the morale-sapping regular doses of chemotherapy. Cassie was told about the psychological benefits that can often result from joining a support group, but she rejected the idea. 'We decided we were stronger being by ourselves,' explained Pierce, whose initial reaction to his wife's illness had been to keep quiet about it. For her sake he wanted everything to be as private as possible, but the news leaked out and the media had a field day. Pierce was furious, but after a few weeks the news that Cassie's early surgery had been a success obliterated most other things from his mind as they settled down together at their lovely home.

Cassie was still extremely weak and Pierce kept his career on hold, devoting all day and every day to looking after his wife and their home. Domesticity had largely passed him by, but according to Cassie, he became a committed house-husband, cleaning, cooking and helping attend to the needs of young Sean. Being tired all the time, Cassie could do little and became depressed, but she said his sense of humour would often lift her spirits. They laughed together when she roused herself one evening to find him slumped in a chair, pouring over a continental cookbook. His dedication and devotion had been absolute, but he could not pretend that life had been anything but difficult. 'But Cassie has a wonderful passion for life,' he told a reporter. 'And the children have handled things extremely well. They have suffered their own "breakdowns", but they're coping. When these things happen you just have to get on with life. We're a very strong family and we can win.'

A further operation in summer 1988 lifted all their spirits and gave some hope for the future. Cassie was not yet cured and would need to continue with her treatment, but significant progress had been made. Because of her illness Pierce had flatly refused even to consider an earlier approach to take the part of Phileas Fogg in the mini-series for television, but when a second chance came along

Cassie did everything she could to get him to take it. Still he was adamant, in spite of his wife's much improved condition. The problem was that a commitment to the role would mean spending a month or two abroad on location work and Pierce again refused, insisting: 'You're much more important than my career.' He was determined to remain with his wife and it was only after much debate, persuasion and with his wife now feeling much better, that he finally, and still somewhat reluctantly, agreed to do the series. The doctors assured him they would keep a close watch on Cassie but, as his wife revealed afterwards, he would call time and time again to make sure she was all right.

By spring 1989 Cassie and Pierce were convinced that the cancer had been conquered. It was an encouraging symbol of his wife's recovery, as much as an early birthday celebration for Charlotte and Christopher, eighteen and seventeen respectively in November that year, when Pierce arranged a surprise party for them all at London's Savoy Hotel in October. The hilarious high-light of the evening, the story goes, was the surprise entrance of a 'cop-o-gram', a male and female police officer who sought to arrest Charlotte and Christopher on a supposed charge of under-age drinking! It was also in a mood of profound relief, as well as a celebration of Cassie's continued progress, that some time later they moved into a magnificent new, seven-bedroom home set in six acres of choice real-estate in fashionable Malibu, overlooking the Pacific Ocean. It was a beautiful, idyllic area in which only the most prosperous and high-profile movie and entertainment super-stars, including Barbra Streisand, Richard Gere and Steven Spielberg, had made their home. Pierce and Cassie loved it. Even if it overstated Pierce's success as a movie actor, it perhaps also reflected for them both their recent, shattering realization of their own mortality. They understood all too well that happiness should be grasped when the opportunities arise and not unnecessarily delayed.

During the difficult and worrying times when Cassie was ill, Pierce propped up his career with fill-in work. Studio and filming commitments always took second place to looking after Cassie, but during the periods when she was doing better, he did manage to fit in a few television projects and, indeed, a couple of substantial movies.

Mister Johnson was Nigeria's first Western feature film and was based on Joyce Cary's novel of the same name. The story follows a young Nigerian clerk who over-reaches himself while helping his colonial master to fulfil an obsessive and overblown ambition to build an elaborate, grandiose road. Bruce Beresford, the Australian director and writer who scored an enormous success with *Driving Miss Daisy* in 1990, directed the new film, which was scripted by the novelist William Boyd from the Cary original. Brosnan played the naïve district officer Harry Rudbeck and looked every inch the army officer, with his erect, military posture and neat moustache. Edward Woodward, who played Sargy Gollup, the luckless, larger-than-life murder victim, and Denis Quilley, who played Rudbeck's older superior, also featured, and the title role was taken by a complete newcomer, English-Nigerian Maynard Eziashi.

The story is set in West Africa in the 1920s and centres on the feckless Rudbeck, who tries to be more English than the English and destroys himself by seeking an easy way out of his problems. As the first international picture to come out of Nigeria, *Mister Johnson* provided long overdue insights into that country in that era. An interesting aspect to the picture included the casting of all the Nigerian parts in just four hours – 150 were selected from the thousands who turned up in the hope of being chosen.

When the film went into production near Josin, northern Nigeria, in January 1990 Brosnan was reluctant to commit to the ten weeks of filming there. However, Cassie persuaded him she would be perfectly all right and that it was important not to let such career opportunities pass. As before, he kept in close and regular contact, but when the picture was released in early 1991 their joint sacrifice must scarcely have seemed worthwhile. Despite a royal premiere in London, *Mr Johnson* was pitifully promoted, managing only a limited release in Britain. Most critics, moreover, found little to interest or excite them. '[It] suffers the same fate as its title character, never coming close to being as important as it desperately wants to be,' said *Variety*. Some writers were more generous, however. One said: 'Deftly acted and directed tragi-comedy of human fallibility and colonial attitudes.' Philip French in *The Observer* offered: 'A very generous, thoughtful and effective movie.' Most telling of all, perhaps, was that the public took little notice, those small numbers who finally were given the opportunity to see it.

The feature film that followed was even more forgettable and seen by even fewer people. *Live Wire*, released in 1992, was an action thriller with Brosnan in the lead role, alongside Ron Silver, Ben Cross and Lisa Eilbacher. It was yet another Brosnan movie that failed to make an impact. Much more important to his career, however, was *The Lawnmower Man*, filmed in 1991. This would be the first positive step towards his ultimate recognition as a major acting talent in films, but Cassie, agonizingly, would not be around to see it.

In early 1991 all the hopes and the renewed zest for living that had grown out of those dark, early days of illness were shattered. Cassie again felt unwell. She knew it, and he feared it. The cancer had returned. But surely, all was not lost? Cassie had been in this situation before and pulled out of it. The improvement in Cassie's physical well-being had brought her and her husband even closer together, and their beautiful home provided the solace and sanctuary that was vital to her recovery. But much as she loved Pierce being with her during these traumatic times, Cassie insisted that he continue to develop his career by not missing out on any opportunity which might be offered.

The Lawnmower Man with its unprepossessing title, initially seemed to offer few prospects for the ambitious Brosnan. Billed as the 'UK's First Virtual Reality Film,' it did, however, break new ground. As its succinct strapline put it: 'God made him simple. Science made him a God.' The strange metamorphosis detailed in the story is well explained by Halliwell: 'A doctor experiments with drugs and computer technology to improve the mind of his retarded gardener, with startling and unforeseen results.'

Brosnan plays the brooding scientist Angelo, who conducts the experiments on his gardener Jobe (Jeff Fahey), raising him, as *Empire* explained, 'from drooling geek with frizzy perm to psychic superbrain with blow-dried bob by directly stimulating his brain.' Or, as one studio source noted: 'Jobe was a gentle soul – until they literally changed his mind! He is then even able to experience the ecstasy and basic pleasure of physical togetherness as any normal human being, purely through the science of virtual reality.'

Despite the inauspicious storyline, the picture did surprisingly good business, proving that public interest in the power of the human mind, a central theme of the picture, can never be underestimated.

The Lawnmower Man opened to British audiences on 5 June 1992. It would become Brosnan's first international movie hit – a cruel irony, for by this time his private world had long since collapsed. He was in deep shock; stranded, bewildered, mourning the wife he had loved so much. It was a body-blow which struck without warning, when, after the family's spirits had been rejuvenated by Cassie's progress, the cancer returned in late spring 1991. According to Brosnan and a number of close friends, Cassie once again faced the pain and anguish with enormous courage. Pierce found the steady deterioration in his wife's condition hard to accept. Frustrated and frightened, he sought desperately to find some cure or at least some relief from suffering for his wife. And he cursed the medical opinion in California, which had given them false hope when she had first gone for consultation with worrying symptoms.

Right now, Cassie's recovery was all that mattered. He again stopped working and devoted all his time to looking after her. Days became tangled, tumbling one after another without form, without outside influences. The world shrank. 'When someone you love and cherish with all your heart has a life-threatening illness, nothing else matters,' he said. 'Whether I am a successful actor isn't important anymore.'

Cassie's inner strength was remarkable, and she remained closely in touch with everything. Pierce drew courage from her fortitude, explaining that they continued to try to get the most out of life, refusing to just sit around and concentrate on her illness. 'And when the pain was unbearable we've just sat down and hugged each other,' he explained. As Cassie's condition worsened, it became normal for them to live a week, a day or two, then just one day at a time, extracting every bit of comfort and pleasure by concentrating on the small things in life that they loved and shared. Hope lingered for a time, and each refused to let go. When that finally slipped away, Pierce stated simply: 'We wept together.'

Both were grateful that Cassie had been able to remain at home, in familiar and loving surroundings, for so long. He told the private nurses he had hired that his wife was drifting in and out of sleep, but whenever she opened her eyes he must be there for her. 'I want her to see my face,' he said. But on 2 December 1991 she entered the Kenneth Norris Jr Cancer Hospital in Los Angeles in severe pain and knowing she had little time to live. Pierce stayed with her, holding her hands, gazing at her, totally exhausted; he would snatch short rests before resuming his vigil.

Thirteen days after she entered hospital, Cassie had her birthday, on Sunday, 15 December. The nurses took Cassie out of her room for a few moments while it was decorated with balloons and streamers. She was then brought back in to be greeted by many of her friends and members of her family. Later, in a quieter moment, Cassie and Pierce in a defining moment spoke honestly with each other, facing the reality of their situation together. Cassie told Pierce that she wanted him to marry again, that she wanted him to have a full and happy life.

The following Sunday, 22 December, Pierce called a local priest and they prayed together. Sheer determination enabled Cassie to see her last two objectives fulfilled – Christmas 1991 and their eleventh wedding anniversary just two days later. That evening, the end inevitable now, Cassie lay there barely conscious, as, in the words Pierce would use later, she began her journey to the other side.

Towards the end Christopher and Charlotte, who had spent a great deal of time with their mother, said their heartrending good-byes so that Pierce and Cassie could be alone together in her final moments. At 10.20, on the morning of Saturday, 28 December 1991, just thirteen days after her fiftieth birthday, she died in her husband's arms.

7
Busy, but No Breakthrough

THE DAYS AFTER CASSIE'S DEATH were nightmarish. The very core of Pierce's being was in serious spasm. Without her the house was empty, his life devoid of meaning. The whole purpose of his existence seemed to have vanished, along with his wife's life. Vivid memories of their life together were consoling, but only made it harder for him to accept that she had gone forever.

There had been plenty of time for him to prepare for Cassie's death. She had been ill for four years and suffered deeply for a good deal of that time, both physically and psychologically. Seldom in all that time, even during the intervals when she was healthier, had Cassie's illness been far from Pierce's mind. The signs had been ominous. Often she would be in great pain. Inwardly he had been trying desperately to condition himself to cope with her death.

At first they had been bright, cheerful, optimistic. But later, quietly, they talked frankly, almost brutally, stripping away as much of the emotion as was humanly possible when faced with the stark reality. Both were dedicated Catholics and appeared to gain strength from their religion. Yet when the dreaded moment arrived, all the preparations and the planning fell apart. His soul was drained, his body emptied; and the void which came with

Cassie's death was real and lasting. For a long time he was numb and had no idea how to begin to fill the emptiness he now experienced. He wasn't sure that he wanted to try to fill even just a part of it. With Cassie everything, life itself, had been so special.

Even the expected can cause deep shock, and while Charlotte and Christopher were old enough to realize the gravity of their mother's condition, there had been no giving up on the possibility of a miracle. Not until life itself had departed. Pierce broke the news to brave six-year-old Sean, his presence a unique symbol of the loving time he and Cassie had spent together. Cassandra Brosnan was cremated, and at a simple private ceremony at a Catholic church in Santa Monica, Pierce, the three children and a small gathering of their closest friends and relatives said their farewells.

A good five years passed before Brosnan could work his way through the trauma of Cassie's death. Essentially a private man not given to blurting out his emotions, he later admitted that he frequently wept during those empty days that followed her death – often quietly on his own and at other times in front of, and indeed with, the children. The family found strength and consolation in their shared grief, and a deeper bond grew between Pierce, Charlotte, Christopher and Sean.

Cassie was very much there in spirit. 'You just have to face the day; keep faith with yourself. I ask myself how I cope every morning. But you see, wherever I go Cassie is always with me.'

For a time he lost his sense of purpose. His ambition disappeared. It took him all his might just to get through each day. He had an urge simply to take off, to be somewhere else. But then he remembered how Cassie, with great emotional strength, had said how she wanted him to continue with his career as an actor and fulfil the dreams they had shared. 'She was a wonderful woman who made me laugh at myself,' Pierce would later explain to the press. It was a feature that particularly appealed to him, because he never appears to have taken himself too seriously.

Meanwhile, *The Lawnmower Man*, which had been completed just before Cassie's death, turned out to be Pierce's first major box-office success on the big screen. Against all the odds it shot into the number 2 slot during the week of its release, eventually grossing $130 million (£90 million) worldwide.

This extremely creditable performance for a fairly low-budget picture surprised many movie insiders. Unusual films are a notorious risk in the industry and *The Lawnmower Man* certainly fitted into that category. In terms of blatant mass appeal it certainly wasn't *The Sound of Music*. Nor James Bond. Producer Edward Simons even went so far as to call it '. . . unique in that it adds a new element, virtual reality, to audiences' proven appreciation for Stephen King's brilliant brand of suspense.' He was perhaps only fractionally off the mark when he predicted just before its release: 'We believe the hi-tech visual concept of the film will dazzle audiences.'

Taken from one of King's less well-known stories, little of the original was left after transferring it to the screen. In fact King was so upset about the way his original story had been mauled and twisted that he took legal action and was granted an injunction forbidding the film's producers from using his name in connection with the film. But purely as a film Kim Newman of *Empire* went so far as to give it a three-star rating, adding: 'It all works surprisingly well with interesting and well integrated unusual effects, some nice human touches and a few genuinely visionary effects.'

Director Brett Leonard explained: 'A technology which creates visually stunning computer simulations known as virtual reality [remember this picture was made in 1991] is used on the town "fool", a simple and sweet soul known as "the lawnmower man". The beauty and ecstasy of his amazing transformation through this process into an intellectually advanced and sophisticated person is offset by the terror we experience when the experiment goes very wrong.' The magazine *Flicks* commented: 'The brilliant obsessed scientist, Dr Lawrence Angelo, played by Pierce Brosnan, never intended to harm his patient. Dominated by The Shop, a mysterious organisation funding his work, Angelo decides to leave his bosses and the hideous experiments he has been performing on chimpanzees, and pursue his own research in a more positive direction. Angelo believes that by using virtual reality and a revolutionary new drug he can offer Jobe Smith, the town's shy gardener who has a mental age of six, a whole new lease of life.'

At first the results are encouraging and astonishing. Jobe rattles through the learning process thirty times faster than normal, but later rebels against the sadistic priest he has been working under and embarks on a torrid affair with the sexiest woman around, Marnie, played by Jenny Wright. In the end just one switched drug and some careful computer programming is all it takes to turn gentle Jobe into a killing machine with a fearsome imagination. The once composed and harmless Jobe becomes bent on settling old scores by killing off in various bizarre ways individuals against whom he had developed a grudge earlier in the story. Angelo eventually struggles to prevent his creation from taking over the world.

Angel Studios, which along with XAOS (pronounced Ka-os) was responsible for the startling effects in *The Lawnmower Man*, had already helped NASA to see satellites in orbit without ever leaving the ground as well as allowing the US Navy to visualize the launch of an SDI missile before one was ever built. In the sphere of general entertainment they had also shown the world a 3D animation of Sea World's most famous killer whale, Shamu, and created a gigantic fire-breathing dragon inspired by a computer game. Said *Film Review* at the time: 'Now Angel Studios have let their imaginations run riot to convey the feverish nightmare world inside Jobe Smith's head.' Pierce was happy to admit that most of the high-tech computer effects were way above his head.

Brosnan was as surprised as everyone by the success of *The Lawnmower Man*. Many years later after his initial triumph as

James Bond, he would explain that it was an independent movie 'made in a warehouse in Santa Monica on a wing and a prayer' with a director (the relatively unknown Brett Leonard) who was 'a clever young fellow who really hit on something'. It would prove to be the one bright interlude in a career that had hit the doldrums. True, he did complete a number of run-of-the-mill television movies in quick succession and was also kept busy making a couple of big-screen movies, the first of which was released in 1993, the other in 1994; but for quite some time, his heart had not really been in the business.

Two of the television movies were based on Alistair Maclean stories. The Scots-born Maclean rather rejected the notion that he was a novelist, preferring to be known as a writer of adventure stories. Many would be made into highly successful movies, most notably *The Guns of Navarone* with Gregory Peck and David Niven in 1961 and the World War Two epic *Where Eagles Dare*, starring Richard Burton and Clint Eastwood in 1969. Though both have been dismissed by some critics as simplistic *Boys Own* romps, both filled cinemas worldwide with adult audiences.

The two television movies based on Maclean's writings that featured Pierce were by no means as well known. *Death Train*, also known as *Detonator*, concerned the adventures of Mike Graham, a weapons expert and a member of the United Nations anti-terror-ist squad. It had a lot of impressive action sequences, and physically Pierce certainly earned his fee. When he is called upon to perform his 'save the world' heroics by stopping a hi-jacked train carrying a nuclear bomb, the effect was almost Bond-like. Much of the film was made in the former Yugoslavia and Pierce took his nine-year-old son Sean with him on location.

Death Train was shown in 1993. A sequel was released in 1995 under the title *Night Watch*, also known as *Detonator 2: Night Watch*. Location work, again in the former Yugoslavia, proved hazardous and arduous, but Pierce was at least working again and these films for television were entertaining enough, if not exactly weighty enough to raise his star status. His co-star in both films was Alexandra Paul, whose face and figure often featured in the glamour scenes in the far more successful *Baywatch* television series.

Sandwiched between *Death Train* and *Night Watch* was *The Broken Chain*, a television film released in 1993 with Eric Schweig, Wes Studi and Buffy Saint-Marie ahead of Pierce in the cast listings; also *Don't Talk to Strangers* (released 1994) in which Pierce had the starring role ahead of Shanna Reed and Terry O' Quinn. Both adventures were eminently forgettable.

By 1993–4 Pierce Brosnan had been in the movie business some fourteen years, had made twelve big-screen movies and taken a leading role in six of them. Yet to the average moviegoer he was still largely unknown. The name was vaguely familiar, but most people would have struggled to name even a couple of his pictures.

Further appearances in *Entangled* (1993), *Mrs Doubtfire*, (released in Britain in January 1994) and *Love Affair*, later that year, also did little to boost his renown among the cinema-going public. Probably the best thing about *Entangled*, from Brosnan's point of view, was that he received a good pay packet for just a few days' work, plus a trip to Paris, where the picture was made. It was a Franco-Canadian production, never regarded as more than a B movie, though some experts suggested that with a bigger budget and more astute handling, this romantic thriller could have done much better. In the event it disappeared rapidly from view. The picture's lead role was taken by Judd Nelson, who had made his film debut at the age of twenty-five in the 1984 movie *Making the Grade* and was then, according to one assessment, beginning to corner the market in 'smugly contentious, troubled young men.'

Love Affair, in 1994, was better, though fared badly with the critics. Here Brosnan appeared alongside major stars Warren

Beatty, Annette Bening, Katherine Hepburn and Gary Shandling, along with Kate Capshaw and Chloe Webb. The film was essentially the second re-make of a movie that had first seen the light of day in 1939. Charles Boyer and Irene Dunne had starred in the highly successful and probably definitive version of a classic Hollywood romantic meeting which goes astray through misunderstandings and a physical accident. Eighteen years later, in 1957, Cary Grant and Deborah Kerr brought the story successfully back to life, in *An Affair to Remember*. The direction had been handled sensitively by Leo McCarey, who had gone into film-making as early as 1918, before joining the famous Hal Roach studio in 1923.

Despite the film's strong pedigree, in particular McCarey's obvious expertise, the latest Brosnan version fell rather flat, proving unable to attract any sizeable audience; but the picture did give a reliable snapshot of Pierce's developing talent for light romantic comedy. It was the unusual *Mrs Doubtfire*, however, released in Britain in January 1994, that notched up Brosnan's profile, not because his role was particularly significant, but just because he was associated with one of the year's most successful movies. It was a comic triumph with the ubiquitous Robin Williams in dazzling form in the title role. Based on Anne Fine's children's classic and directed by *Home Alone*'s Chris Columbus, the simple plot was transformed by Williams's talent into something extraordinary.

After a messy divorce the unemployed Daniel Hillard, played by Robin Williams, is permitted to see his three children just once a week. He loves them dearly and is devastated at not being able to see them more often. His estranged workaholic wife Miranda, played by Sally Field, has advertised for a housekeeper who can also cope with her brood while she is carrying out her executive duties at the office. Robin Williams sees an opportunity to get closer to his children, so applies for the job and his wife takes him on.

But how? Because when he goes for interview he arrives as Mrs Doubtfire, an ample, benevolent lady with a soft, lilting Scottish accent; she's warm, generous of spirit and obviously devoted to children. They love her and take to her instantly. As *Flicks* reported at the time: 'Robin Williams has run the gamut of comic brilliance, both visual and even purely vocal, but nothing will have quite prepared audiences for his laughter-making versatility in this movie.' The picture is hilarious: Williams' ample form sparks audiences into laughter whenever he sails into view. As one review put it: 'Not since Dustin Hoffman in *Tootsie* has so much latex been used so well as on Williams playing Mrs Doubtfire, a wonderful old battleaxe let loose into the lives of a chic workaholic divorcee (Sally Field) and her three children.'

Mrs Doubtfire was a major success in the United States, clocking up in excess of $200 million at the box office to become one of the biggest hits of the nineties. Brosnan's role is tiny compared with Williams's bravura performance, but simply being part of such a blockbuster, which caught the imagination of such a broad cross-section of filmgoers, was in itself a good morale-booster for Brosnan. He admitted after the picture had been released: 'Until now only one of my films, *The Lawnmower Man*, has made any kind of impact.' He explained that he had turned down television work to be more selective and to wait for the right role to come along. Securing the right role was important, even if it cost him financially. He said shortly afterwards: 'But getting the part in *The Lawnmower Man* made it worthwhile. I think this film is truly a turning point.'

In *Mrs Doubtfire*, Brosnan plays Stu, Miranda's slick new boyfriend, the possessor of a swanky car and a smooth line in conversation. He wastes little time in trying to advance his relationship with Miranda, but in a hilarious scene the puritanical Mrs Doubtfire will have none of it. Superficially, Stu is seen as a handsome rogue, but Brosnan maintained that he came through as a nice guy, a genuinely sympathetic character.

Making *Mrs Doubtfire* was an enjoyable experience for Brosnan, and studio gossip had it that he and Williams got on well together. 'It was great fun,' said Brosnan looking back on the experience. By all accounts both men improvised, Pierce claiming that all his scenes with Robin carried a good deal of invented dialogue. 'The ad-libs didn't bother me,' said Brosnan, adding: 'It was great to work with Robin, but a big challenge.'

But the even bigger challenge, to be cast as the lead in a high-profile movie, seemed to be as far away as ever, while his early ambition to play James Bond had surely disappeared forever. By now Timothy Dalton's debut as James Bond in *The Living Daylights* in 1987 had raked in $191 million, the third biggest box-office receipts for a Bond movie and beaten only by *Moonraker* in 1979 ($203 million) and *For Your Eyes Only* in 1981 ($195 million), both featuring Roger Moore. And Dalton's position seemed to be consolidated, when he was cast almost automatically in the following Bond movie, *Licence to Kill*, which would be released in 1989. In fact rumours had it, though the actor himself refuted the suggestion, that the script had been written with Dalton's distinctive characterization in mind.

Any fading hopes that Brosnan clung to would soon be abandoned, as bitter litigation played out in the American courts carried the real threat that James Bond might soon complete his final mission.

8

Bond – Second Time Around

TUESDAY, 1 JUNE 1994, was the day Pierce Brosnan heard officially that he would be the next James Bond. He reportedly took a very early morning phone call at his California home, telling him the job was his. A week later, at the Regent Hotel in London's Marylebone Road, he appeared before the world's press as the first new 007 in eight years. His unveiling was no surprise. Aged forty-one, Brosnan was such a hot favourite with the public that bookmakers had already stopped taking bets on the identity of the new 007. But on that momentous day he certainly did not look the part. Into a room packed with journalists, photographers and officials he emerged with long hair and a healthy growth of beard. He was about to disappear on location abroad for a television adaptation of *Robinson Crusoe*. But when he spoke he proved he was no stranger to the character he was soon to portray: 'I would like to see what is beneath the surface of this man, what drives him on, what makes him a killer. I think we will peel back the onion skin, as it were,' he said. His natural charm and understated demeanour went down well with the press. They liked his self-deprecating sense of humour, but he admitted later that he had been terribly nervous.

Later he spoke more about how he saw his own particular James

Bond. 'Some of the original concept of the character had perhaps been lost or changed over the years,' he explained. 'There's a lethal quality to him; he's a trained killer. He'll be charming and sophisticated of course, but ruthless also.'

Brosnan's comments might well have seemed a trifle presumptuous for an actor whose CV was not all that impressive. For at the time James Bond was probably the most coveted role in the business. Certainly it had the highest public profile. It would have been a major coup for many of cinema's top-ranking stars. For Brosnan it was a rocket-power boost to a career that had shown little significant development in six years, *The Lawnmower Man* in 1992 being the notable exception to a string of pedestrian roles in a run of largely second-rate movies.

'I certainly wasn't waiting for James Bond to come back into my life,' he claimed. Nor, it appears, was he at first all that optimistic about securing the part. He remembered he had progressed this far before and had done little in the intervening years to prove himself a worthy candidate. He was also honest enough with himself to realize that he was now eight years older, a long time for an action-man like James Bond. 'But when something comes into your life for a second time it carries a certain significance. I couldn't say no. It was like unfinished business and I had to get it out of the way,' he explained.

From the start the new James Bond movie was beset with difficulties and frustrations. The finance was in position; no problem on that score. But the fears were real that Tim Dalton's portrayal in *Licence to Kill* some six years before could well be 007's swansong. Before anything could happen there was (a) a forbidding legacy behind 007's long absence from the screen that had to be cleared up; (b) Tim Dalton decided he did not want to play Bond anymore; (c) a new enemy for James to overcome was needed, since Russia was now a democracy and those trusty old plots about eliminating Communist agents behind the Iron Curtain wouldn't wash anymore; and (d) when Broccoli and Co. were almost set to start, they found that Bond's traditional film-making home was already hard at work doing other things and not available.

After Ian Fleming's world-famous character had first been consigned to celluloid in *Dr No* in October 1962 a new 007 adventure appeared every year for the next three years. Never in Bond history would fans have to wait more than two-and-a-half years for his return and from 1979 James Bond had obediently turned up every other year – *Moonraker* in 1979, *For Your Eyes Only* (1981), *Octopussy* (1983), *A View to a Kill* (1985), *The Living Daylights* (1987), and *Licence to Kill* (1989).

Now Bond's six-and-a-half year absence was beginning to look ominous. No wonder Pierce had put his vision to one side. You can't live your life on dreams, nor build a career on what might have been. Would James Bond ever return? A protracted and increasingly bitter legal battle between Albert 'Cubby' Broccoli's Eon Productions, which owned the 007 franchise, and MGM/UA, the studio which funded the films, was at the core of the long delay in bringing Bond into action again. Not until early 1993 was Broccoli confident that he had safeguarded the Bond franchise and was able to push ahead with his plans.

Meanwhile, Timothy Dalton, who was rumoured to have been contracted for three Bond movies, grew impatient with the endless delays, and quit. His departure was amicable. Few had seen him as the natural successor to Connery and Moore, though he had his supporters, and his first appearance as Bond in *The Living Daylights* had broken many box-office records in numerous countries. His second Bond movie however, *Licence to Kill*, was something of a let-down, with worldwide receipts dropping to $156 million, but which built up reasonably well over a much longer period of time. His premature and unexpected departure, however, was not seen as a serious problem.

Brosnan was widely considered to be ideal, but again he came perilously close to missing out on the great opportunity. It was an action replay of the Remington Steele affair, but this time with a happier ending. The surprise success of *The Lawnmower Man* had prompted a follow-up. Brosnan had actually agreed terms, but fortunately this time had not signed a contract and no legal action was forthcoming. In fact the sequel went ahead without him in the main part, but proved to be a commercial and artistic flop.

At the same time the framework of *GoldenEye*, the agreed title of the latest and seventeenth film in the official Bond series, was being assembled. Having produced fifteen of the Bond adventures in as many years the astute and vastly experienced Cubby Broccoli, now 74 years old, decided it was time to ease back a little. His stepson Michael G. Wilson and his 34-year-old daughter Barbara Broccoli took over as producers.

Both had plenty of experience in the business. Wilson had been with Eon Productions since 1972, having joined in a legal/administrative capacity. He was assistant producer on *The Spy Who Loved Me* and executive producer on *Moonraker*, *For Your Eyes Only* and *Octopussy*. He had produced (with Albert Broccoli) the three most recent Bond films, *A View to a Kill*, *The Living Daylights* and *Licence to Kill*. He had also co-written many of the Bond movies.

Barbara Broccoli was head of the Cubby Broccoli company, Danjaq Inc. For a number of years she had also worked in the production and casting departments of Eon Productions. Barbara had majored in motion picture and television communications at Loyola University in Los Angeles, California, and had been an assistant director on *Octopussy* and *A View to a Kill*, and associate producer (with Tom Pevsner) on the last two Bond adventures, *The Living Daylights* and *Licence to Kill*.

GoldenEye took its name from that of Ian Fleming's home in Jamaica, where he first began writing the James Bond novels in 1952. Albert Broccoli had set Michael France to work researching and writing an original story as early as May 1993. France had written the smash-hit action-thriller *Cliffhanger*, starring Sylvester Stallone, and later worked on a big-screen adaptation of the popular comic book *The Fantastic Four* for top-flight producer Chris Columbus. France's background research for *GoldenEye* took him to Moscow and St Petersburg, where he was able to observe the current state of the military and intelligence circles in Russia. He also had the rare opportunity, as an American, to go inside KGB headquarters in Moscow and tour military and nuclear facilities. He was also able to familiarize himself with the latest advances in espionage tools and tactics, as well as hi-tech weaponry, including the electro-magnetic pulse generator.

At this point Brosnan had not yet been cast as the new James Bond. France said at the time: 'It was sort of generally assumed that it would be Tim [Dalton], so I tried to write it with him in mind, a lot of physical action, some emotional intensity with double agent Alec Trevelyan [the role eventually taken by Sean Bean], and not too much humour.' Michael France's story was then reworked into a screenplay by British writer Jeffrey Caine. Much later, Bruce Feirstein, whose work was known to Barbara Broccoli, was brought in to add some important final touches in preparation for shooting.

Communism, Russia and the Iron Curtain could no longer serve as the collective enemy. They had given way to a new world order, and in the final script political power plays were replaced by ruthless struggles for profit. But with Bond, only so much can change. 'The war had changed ... but the warriors remain the same,' explained early publicity. '*GoldenEye* was set firmly in the present day, its swiftly changing political patterns turning old opponents into new best friends; and allies into deadly enemies.'

One gigantic problem still remained. Britain's Pinewood Studios was the traditional home for the shooting of James Bond films. All of them had been made there. But when the time came to set up Pinewood for the new shoot it was already fully booked. Ironically, the studio had been signed up for the making of the new movie, *First Knight*, starring original Bond, Sean Connery. An exhaustive and somewhat panic-stricken search for alternative accommodation was undertaken, in Europe, Canada and the United States, but in the end the right spot was identified almost on Pinewood's doorstep.

Curiously, however, as early as March 1994, behind the scenes at the Oscar ceremonies in Los Angeles, Broccoli was reported to have made contact with Screen Wales, a publicly sponsored organization charged with promoting film-making in the principality. The producer wanted to sound out the possibility of making *GoldenEye* at Brawdy, a decommissioned RAF base in Pembrokeshire. With ten enormous hangars and hundreds of acres of land, it appeared on the face of it to be an ideal location. But it never happened. Later rumours suggested that Broccoli had fleetingly toyed with the idea when he was looking at the possibility of Sir Anthony Hopkins, born in Port Talbot and a keen supporter of Screen Wales, playing Bond's adversary in the new film.

It was executive producer Tom Pevsner and associate producer Anthony Waye who finally discovered the existence of an abandoned wartime airplane factory and airfield on a 2,860-acre site at Leavesden in Hertfordshire, not all that distant from Pinewood Studios in neighbouring Buckinghamshire and conveniently close to London. After agreeing a formal one-year lease with owners Rolls-Royce, the world-famous company gave permission for Eon Productions to make whatever alterations were necessary to convert it into a working film studio.

The production team handed on the challenge to Delta Doric, the company who had rebuilt the original 007 stage in record time after a devastating fire in 1984. Within just five months Leavesden's cavernous space was transformed into Europe's newest film facility with 1.25 million square feet of interior space

94

– as much as the whole of the Pinewood Studios' facilities put together. Five working sound stages were constructed, along with a carpentry shop, prop shop, paint shop, model shop, a special effects stage, dressing rooms and office space. The transformation constituted a minor miracle of organization, dedication and application. The enormous backlot, with two clear skylines, could support several major productions simultaneously.

Brosnan might perhaps have wondered just what he was getting into, for much of the industry had doubts about Bond's relevance in the nineties and felt that the whole concept was in decline. After all, Bond and his exploits were the stuff of sheer fantasy – whether he could be sustained in the more hard-nosed realities of the modern world was anybody's guess. Surely even less likely to be tolerated was his playful chauvinism towards women.

Brosnan said he never worried about any of that, for doubtless some changes would be made as a nod to the passing of time. And certainly, the prospect of a new James Bond movie after such a long absence did catch the public imagination, particularly since the picture would reveal a reincarnated James in the form of the young, handsome and now widely recognized man-of-the-moment Pierce Brosnan. (He was the sixth actor to play the role, incidentally, if you count David Niven in the non-Eon production of *Casino Royale*.) Many observers agreed Brosnan was the obvious choice, and his casting gave the new film an additional impetus.

'To be honest there was never anybody else in the frame,' director Martin Campbell admitted to *What's On In London* some time later. He saw one or two other actors, just in case, but he was never really in doubt about choosing Brosnan as the new Bond. In truth this was not the entire story. Brosnan did not get the role simply by default. Since being seen as the obvious and agreed choice of Bond eight years before – a very long time in the movie business – when he was riding high as television's glamorous Remington Steele, he was seen to have made little noticeable headway on the

95

big screen. He was no longer the automatic choice and his selection was only confirmed after a number of meetings had taken place between Broccoli and the film's producers, daughter Barbara and stepson Michael Wilson.

But in advance of the official announcement it was all part of the game to let the media rumours spread, and all kinds of names were linked to the coveted role. Mel Gibson was probably the most famous name to be tossed into the ring. Broccoli had reportedly offered him £10 million to take over as James Bond. Others were apparently screen-tested. Kenneth Branagh was probably the least likely candidate; Hugh Grant somehow didn't seem right either. In the early days of the project there had been doubts about whether Pierce would say yes to the role. He had previously hinted that he would find it hard to play Bond now. The character had been returning to the screens for a long time, and whether he had a long-term future was open to question. It would have damaged Brosnan's professional career, particularly at this crunch point, to be part of a monumental flop. But this latest Bond movie was set to break new ground in a number of important ways.

For a start it was the first Bond movie to be made in the 1990s, so some changes were expected – and necessary. But were some of the changes too severe, too extreme? Lois Maxwell as Miss Moneypenny, the loyal, workaholic secretary to M, who had a sneaking passion for James Bond, was replaced by a younger and more liberated girl of the 1990s, in the form of Samantha Bond. This aptly named female Bond had recently appeared in the Royal Shakespeare Company's presentations of *A Winter's Tale* and *As You Like It*, although she was also experienced in more popular television programmes like *Inspector Morse*, *Rumpole of the Bailey* and in the radio drama adaptation of *Romeo and Juliet*. In her new role she continued to flirt rather passively with Bond, and still had that special feeling for him – not entirely sexual, of course, nor wholly platonic either.

96

Smooth & smart as the front man in the highly successful television series *Remington Steele* (1982–7), in which Brosnan co-starred with Stephanie Zimbalist. Yet in 1986 the series thwarted his long-held ambition to play James Bond

Keen to build his reputation in big-screen movies, Brosnan co-starred with Lesley-Anne Down in the 1986 released *Nomads,* about a French anthropologist involved with a group of scary street people in Los Angeles

Working with established star Michael Caine in the 1987 espionage-thriller, *The Fourth Protocol,* was seen as a major move forward in Brosnan's burgeoning screen career. It was his fourth big screen movie

As a battling local debt collector keeping crooked developers at bay in *Taffin* (1988)

Battling again as an English army officer serving in India in *The Deceivers* (1988)

Keen to escape the small screen, Brosnan nonetheless featured as Phileas Fogg in the TV mini-series based on the Jules Verne classic, *Around the World in Eighty Days* (1989). Also starring Peter Ustinov as Detective Fix, it achieved impressive ratings

In the TV movie *Victim of Love* (1991)
with JoBeth Williams and Virginia Madsen,
but the year belonged to the big screen
with the release of *Mr Johnson*, in which Brosnan co-starred with Edward Woodward. He
was cast as a visionary British officer, complete with braces and a moustache, in West Africa
in the 1920s, but the film was not a major success

Live Wire (1992) was an inconsequential action-thriller which did little to advance Brosnan's career as a movie actor, despite appearing with established actors Ron Silver and Ben Cross

Against all expectations the British-produced movie, *The Lawnmower Man* (1992), blending virtual reality with author Stephen King's special brand of suspense, became Brosnan's first big-screen box-office success. It reached no. 2 in its first week in the US and grossed almost £90 million ($130 million) worldwide. Pierce is seen as Dr Lawrence Angelo, aiming to improve the intelligence of Jobe (Jeff Fahey) with virtual reality and drugs

In 1993 Brosnan continued to make money from TV movies, although *Broken Chain* made little impact. Pierce played an Irishman in eighteenth-century America

Mrs Doubtfire (1993) was an outstanding triumph for its star Robin Williams, and a joy for Brosnan, though cast in the fairly minor role as the ultra-smooth new boyfriend of wife and mother Miranda (Sally Field)

With Annette Bening in the 1994 remake of the classic Hollywood romantic movie *Love Affair*. The film was not a great success, even though Brosnan appeared alongside major stars Warren Beatty and Katherine Hepburn

Pierce in 1994, stripped-off, fired up and all set for the starring role in CBS's new TV drama, *Robinson Crusoe*

The big breakthrough: Brosnan as Bond in the 1995 blockbuster *GoldenEye*. He was widely considered to be ideal for what was probably the most coveted, and certainly the highest profile, role in the business. The picture smashed box-office records internationally and grossed in excess of $350 million

(Brosnan still photograph from the motion picture *GoldenEye* © 1995 Danjaq, LLC and United Artists Corporation. All rights reserved)

Pierce continued to be in demand with the release of no fewer than four mainstream movies in 1997, including his second appearance as Bond. In the Tri-Star picture *The Mirror Has Two Faces* he appeared alongside superstar Barbra Streisand, with Jeff Bridges also in the cast

Mars Attacks!, released in 1997, was admired for its technical brilliance. In this all-star mad cap spoof about an alien invasion of planet earth, Brosnan appears as the pipe-smoking Professor Donald Kessler alongside Sarah Jessica Parker as Nathalie Lake

A more extreme metamorphosis was the fate of M himself, Bond's cantankerous superior at HQ. He was to undergo a change of gender between pictures. Since the start of the Bond movies back in 1962 Bernard Lee had steadily acquired the status of the definitive M, appearing in the first nine Bond films. Then from *Octopussy* in 1983, the character had been played by Robert Brown, reprising the role three times. But for *GoldenEye* the esteemed British stage and screen actress Dame Judi Dench took over the role. It was a courageous manoeuvre, but a high-risk break with Bond tradition. Would Bond's legion of tenacious and possessive fans accept James having to take orders from a female? Even as recently as 1994 it was a valid question in commercial terms.

But the experienced skills of Judi Dench would work the miracle. As Lee Pfeiffer and Dave Worrall in *The Essential Bond* put it: 'Judi Dench quieted the cynics with a dynamic, no-nonsense approach to the role.' And later: 'With Dench in the role, the relationship takes on a whole new mystique. There is still mutual respect between the two, but it is understated and therefore all the more meaningful.'

Dench said, as the movie neared completion, 'I was absolutely delighted when I got the call because I've been a huge Bond fan for years and Bernard Lee, who originally played the part, was a great friend of mine. I can now refer to myself as a Bond woman.' She added: 'I enjoyed playing M, who adopts quite a tough line in this movie but, then again, how would you become head of MI6 by being anything but tough?' Brosnan remembered the line uttered by M that seemed destined to become a Bond classic. She turns to 007: 'I think you are a sexist, misogynist dinosaur,' she proclaims in that disdainful way that is pure Dench. Reminded of the scene Pierce laughed. 'She just nails me,' he said. 'The line adds a distinctly different slant to Bond's relationship with M. As an actor, working with Judi was certainly one of the highlights of the movie for me. She's a magnificent actress, a great lady and a wonderful person.'

Dench showed how important is the casting of a minor, albeit pivotal role in a major movie. As M she completed all she had to do in the picture in just two days' work on the set. But it could have seriously affected the extent of *GoldenEye*'s success if she had been less convincing and audiences had not accepted her in the role.

The Bond evergreen, Desmond Llewelyn, then an octogenarian, returned to play the ingenious Q for the fifteenth time. By now he seemed almost as indispensable to a Bond movie as the hero himself. His ability to deliver the most absurd lines with consummate conviction is a hallmark; in *GoldenEye* he displays a priceless ten seconds of pure artistry when he snatches out of Bond's hands what we all assume to be the latest killer gadget, disguised as an ordinary sandwich. 'Don't touch that!' he yells, startling audiences almost out of their seats. 'It's my lunch.' His exasperated admonition, 'Grow up, 007,' simply had to be included, and it was. The phrase has now been directed to every actor who has played Bond over the last three decades.

And of course, no Bond movie would ever be complete without those ubiquitous Bond girls. This time they appeared in the shapely forms of a former supermodel from Holland with strong ambitions to secure a Hollywood career, Famke Janssen, and a Polish-born pop star from Sweden, Izabella Scorupco.

As *femme fatale* Xenia Onatopp, Janssen, in only her fifth movie appearance, was a fetching and impressive villainess whose speciality is squeezing men to death between her thighs during love-making. Would you believe, Bond manages to escape the consequences of the former while . . . well, they don't call him James Bond for nothing. His punchline in the film seems so close to Brosnan's own sense of quiet humour . . . 'she always did enjoy a good squeeze.' Izabella Scorupco, as the beautiful 'good girl'

Natalya, was making her movie debut in this picture. As a computer ace on Bond's side caught up in the search for *GoldenEye*, she is destined to meet a rather sticky end.

But this time round even the Bond girls have changed. 'They're much tougher and much better actresses,' claimed director Martin Campbell. Brosnan explained: 'Women are still an integral part of a Bond movie. But of course you have to make changes. There's still the sexuality, a sensuality about them.' But now they have attitude, they have opinions. Both girls are strong characters. And both were ideally cast.'

Janssen said the villain was definitely her part, claiming that the way she looked prevented her from taking 'housewife, girlfriend' type of roles. On the other hand, Scorupco (Natalya) didn't have Hollywood in her sights. As the good Russian girl who teams up with Bond to expose the post-Soviet baddies, she too was ideal in the role.

Backed by a $50 million budget, filming began on 16 January 1994. Considering all the problems this was a remarkable achievement, being only four months after the original scheduled date for action to begin. Pierce occupied a rented house in Hampstead, north London, and was chauffeur-driven to the studios each day. A twelve-hour working day, generally six days a week, at Leavesden, was not unusual, and to ensure an early, prompt start on the set Brosnan would be out of bed and on his way heading out of London in the dawning light. The shooting schedule was spread over five months. Beneath those cool looks and calm exterior, Brosnan seemed revitalized. That first day of shooting would become a defining moment in his career. He was excited and stimulated, but it was also a day for nerves and tension. 'It was a huge responsibility,' he admitted, and who could argue with that? For here was not just a new Bond movie with a different storyline, new presentation and new stunts. This was also a completely new James Bond.

Pierce was all too aware of how everything rested on the new Bond – comparisons would be made and old loyalties defended. He was very much on his own. He admitted that appearing alongside such talent and experience, so evident both in front of the cameras and behind the scenes, was scary. 'I tried to keep Bond simple and exciting,' he explained. He would concentrate on one day at a time. 'It's important to stay relaxed,' he would say. 'Things can easily get too intense, but there was also the wonderful buzz from doing something you really want to do.'

Making the movie was exciting, fun, hard work, tiring, but his childhood dream had come true. In the midst of all the responsibility that comes with such an important role, it is fascinating to consider that just six short words, and how he should say them, dominated his mind.

Picture the scene. The location is the principality of Monaco and the action is a perilous car race down the narrow, twisting mountain roads above the Grand Corniche. It is to be the first provocative encounter between Bond, driving the classic Aston Martin DB5, and the mysterious Xenia Onatopp in a fiery red Ferrari. The two meet face to face in the elegant Monte Carlo casino, where 007 then must utter his now classic line . . .

These words are every bit as enshrined in the folklore of the screen hero as the name Bond itself, or 007. They even claim their rightful place in the history of the movies. Said Pierce at the time: 'Of course, you do think about it. I mean, it's one of those lines that are in people's consciousness, like "to be or not to be". You find yourself brushing your teeth in the morning going, "The name is Bond, James Bond." In the end I had to have the confidence to just stand there and deliver; you look 'em in the eye and keep it simple.'

A Bond film is a global enterprise, and while much of the picture was shot at the Leavesden headquarters, actors, crews and ancillary workers and staff travelled to faraway places on location. Puerto

Rico and Switzerland, St Petersburg and the French Riviera – all were used as authentic backdrops in what was a highly complex operation. *GoldenEye* was the first ever James Bond adventure that had been allowed to film inside the former Soviet Union, an intriguing fact when set against the ban which that country had imposed on the general release there of all sixteen previous Bond movies.

It was in the harbour of Monte Carlo that scenes were shot on the French Navy's newest frigate, *La Fayette*. In keeping with the hi-tech nature of the movie, the advanced helicopter dubbed the Tiger was seen on the deck of the warship. This was the first of five prototypes built by France and Germany and capable of performing a once-impossible vertical loop.

The Contra Dam near Locarno in Switzerland was chosen for one of the most breathtaking stunts ever achieved on film. Stunt coordinator Simon Crane and stuntman Wayne Michaels orchestrated an astounding bungee jump off the top of the dam, the world record for a leap against a fixed object – all 750 concrete feet of it. Brosnan, who insisted on doing many of his stunts, opted out of that one, which provided a spectacular opening to the movie.

Crane's talent and courage were well known to Brosnan. One of the forty films he had been involved in was *The Fourth Protocol* eight years earlier, in which he doubled for Brosnan in a stunt. He was also admired as the stunt coordinator on the Mel Gibson hit, *Braveheart*.

The film's thrilling climax was partially filmed on the sun-drenched island of Puerto Rico, where the world's largest spherical radio telescope at Arecibo doubled for Trevelyan's satellite dish, aimed at creating a worldwide cataclysm. It also served as the backdrop for the final life-and-death confrontation between two evenly matched adversaries: agent 007 and former agent 006. Simon Crane, whose amazing stunts had been seen in earlier Bond movies, worked extensively with Brosnan and Sean Bean to choreograph the suspense-filled battle.

101

By general consensus *GoldenEye* was seen as the most thrilling Bond film yet.

But not all locations were foreign, or glamorous. A good deal of the action purporting to take place in St Petersburg was shot at Leavesden. Special sets were constructed to represent the MI6 headquarters, the Severnays control station, the opulent Monte Carlo casino, the nerve gas plant infiltrated by 007 and 006 in the film's opening sequences, a lavish Turkish bath and spa in St Petersburg's Grand Hotel Europa, Trevelyan's ultra-modern satellite control room, as well as Valentin's lair, where he is confronted by his old nemesis, James Bond.

Pierce was not alone in admiring what was perhaps the most impressive of all the sets – the re-creation of the streets of St Petersburg on Leavesden's huge backlot for the film's spectacular chase sequence. Though much of the actual chase would be completed on location in St Petersburg, the degree of destruction anticipated made shooting some portions in the historic city impossible. For more than six weeks over 170 workman toiled to complete this magnificent set. Sixty-two miles of scaffolding were used to support the fabricated street, which was constructed over an area of two acres. Said producer Michael Wilson: 'The street was 510 feet long and we ran a tank up and down it for a month. But I think the results were fantastic – we got a good chase out of it.' And for the sequences showing a semi-derelict Soviet military rail depot ... read the picturesque Nene Valley narrow-gauge steam railway, near not-quite-so-exotic Peterborough.

Brosnan energetically worked through the sometimes complicated, physically arduous stunts and the many athletic sequences. He had hardened and improved his normally lean and athletic physique and increased his strength with a carefully prepared, challenging routine of weight training. He was the star and accepted the responsibility gladly, though to be the new boy bringing Bond back to life after an absence of more than six years cannot have been without its stresses. Yet when asked if he was trying to bring something new to Bond, his response seemed eminently sensible: 'That's the big question. I'm bringing Brosnan to Bond, though there are certain Bond characteristics that you have to adhere to. He likes women, he is a killer, he is a man who is highly trained.' But is that like Brosnan? 'No, Brosnan is an actor,' he replied. 'Brosnan can hopefully fill those shoes. My job is to create an illusion, a character. One aspect I'd like to see in the character is a certain vulnerability. Heroes have changed cinematically since the days of Sean Connery doing Bond.'

To say that meant giving Bond additional angst, as someone at the time suggested, would probably make Brosnan wince; but certainly that kind of extra dimension, whatever you wish to call it, is exactly what Mel Gibson so successfully gave his hero in *Lethal Weapon* – and what Brosnan hoped to bring to Bond.

He felt that modern audiences wanted a hero more on the lines of those created by the Harrison Fords and Mel Gibsons of this world. 'The characters these men have created have something which makes them more accessible – and yet they are heroes on a grand scale,' he told *Empire*. He later admitted to being filled with trepidation as to whether he could do it. He realized all too well that he was taking on a movie legacy. But the excitement was there. 'I didn't want to screw the damn thing up. I'm a big fan of Bond and in any case it's not a job you take lightly,' he recalled. 'There's an audience out there of thirty-three years standing, so it's a big responsibility.'

Though certain aspects of Bond films cannot change, Brosnan did well to bring a new sophistication to Bond's unique way with women. Connery's technique had been masculine and dominant. Moore had been more light-hearted, almost flippant. Brosnan's technique was in a sense more calm, more controlled. He was, in fact, cool; and here he gave credit to costume designer Lindy Hemmings and others who made the new Bond 'correct for his time'. Brosnan confirmed: 'They gave me an elegant yet modern look . . . nothing aggressively trendy. And the script was very tight, very sharp and very funny. All this gave me added incentive and confidence in taking on the role.' Somehow he was able to project a certain sincerity, and in so doing, seemed a little less 'comic-book' than his predecessors. But in the end Bond is still Bond, certainly in terms of that animal-like desire that exists between 007 and whoever the females might be, friend or foe.

Brosnan conceded that the public had high expectations, and when a film has been in the planning stages for six years the pressure is great. 'It spurs you on,' he said. 'It makes you want to give your best. In any case I've had a good feeling about this film from the start.' The hints of tension brought on by heavy responsibility were hardly surprising because, as he pointed out, it takes a lot of courage to play James Bond. 'He comes with so much baggage, such a great sense of tradition. It's the number one franchise in the movies.'

Director Martin Campbell added: 'If you look back at all the various actors who have played Bond, they've all brought entirely different characteristics to the role. Now we've got Pierce, who has all the right qualities. He is not only a very fine actor, but is wonderful with the humour, fantastic at action and is a terrific looking guy with a real classiness to him.'

Comparisons with former Bonds were inevitable, and Brosnan was rated highly. Pierce had always admired the Sean Connery Bond, while Roger Moore had also stamped his own mark on the role. Any comparisons were bound to have little real meaning, even if emotionally they were important; after all, both Connery and Moore had played 007 several times, enough to take over and develop the character, whereas Brosnan's performance was a debut.

The fact that the Bond role had slipped through Brosnan's fingers in 1986 perhaps turned out in hindsight to be a blessing in disguise. 'In those few years Pierce gained important maturity, physically, facially and as an actor, making him a much more convincing choice at the time of *GoldenEye*,' said a studio executive. When interviewed during the making of the film Brosnan agreed: 'It's better that it happened now,' he confirmed. 'It feels right now; it never felt quite right then.' He was, at forty-one, eight years older than when he was first approached. One noted film buff added: 'With his chiselled features and suave manner, Pierce Brosnan was born to play Bond.'

There was little doubt that securing the Bond role was deeply emotional for Brosnan, though in public he kept professionally cool. But in the more cloistered company of his close friends, and particularly his family, the feeling ran deeper. They felt it was a triumph for Cassie as well as for themselves, and Charlotte, Christopher and Sean shared Pierce's own delight and pride in achieving such a long-held ambition. Christopher in fact was a little closer to the action than Charlotte or Sean, his father having pulled a few strings to enable him to be one of the two production runners on the movie.

James Bond is by far the longest-running and also the most popular film franchise of all time. But it had now been more than thirty long years since the release of *Dr No* and the character's recent enforced six-year absence could well have dropped him into an obscurity from which too few people wanted him to recover. Nothing lasts for ever, and times had changed. Therefore Bond had to change, too. The challenge for the makers of *GoldenEye* was deciding just how much change the public would expect or accept.

Any change would be a risk, but to make no changes would be an even greater risk. There were few doubts among the moviemakers that Brosnan was the man for the job. Other cast changes were generally accepted as being right. But whatever alterations were made elsewhere, one crucial feature of all the Bond movies must be retained, expanded even, and made even more visually exciting than before. We are talking about the movies' magical pantheon of dramatic, high-flying, eye-widening, gigantic, hypnotic stunts, not to forget those hair-raising and extraordinary 'set pieces'. The script, however good, had to incorporate that. And it did, with Bond occupying, as ever, the role of superhero with a one-man mission to save the world.

An ultra-secret NATO Tiger helicopter has been skyjacked. A space weapons research centre inside the Arctic Circle has been destroyed. Bond is briefed by the newly appointed M, equipped with the latest technical wizardry by Q and sent to the new Russia, in order to penetrate the local arms mafia and locate the culprit.

This seemingly straightforward assignment brings him face to face with his past. Nine years before, during a mission at a top secret Soviet nerve-gas facility, Bond and his close friend, Secret Service contemporary Alex Trevelyan (agent 006) were detected and trapped. For once Bond hesitates and is forced to decide between saving the mission or his partner's life. He opted for the former and assumed Trevelyan was executed by Soviet General Ourumov.

His latest assignment sets him on the trail of the elusive Janus, a twisted genius plotting to destroy the information superhighway, and send the world's economy back to the Stone Age by accessing an extraordinary device known only as GoldenEye. Advance publicity tempted: 'Once again, from St Petersburg to the Caribbean, 007 is forced to break all the rules in a deadly game of cat and mouse. Blind frontal assault. Zero back-up. No pre-planned escape route.' James discovers that GoldenEye may well be in the possession of Janus, an unseen organized-crime operator active in the new Russia. Even more alarming is the realization that Janus is actually his old friend Trevelyan (played by Sean Bean). He was not executed after all, and is now plotting with his supposed executioner, Ourumov, to financially cripple London and then cover up the crime by firing the GoldenEye over the city. Helped by former Russian computer programmer Natalya Simonova (Isabella Scorupco), Bond discovers Trevelyan's secret hideaway in Cuba, and in a fight to the death destroys his former colleague and saves the world. A surprising Bond ally was popular British television actor Robbie Coltrane, whose powerful performance in *Cracker* had won him an international reputation. His character, Valentin Zukovsky, head of the Russian mafia in St Petersburg, is a former enemy of Bond. The two form an uneasy alliance for mutual benefit.

With Connery so universally accepted as the Bond that everybody loved, and, given the chance, would perhaps not have changed, Pierce Brosnan was certainly treading in fabled footsteps in *GoldenEye*. He explained, 'People are going to be waiting to see the new James Bond and that's what gives the film an edge; that's what makes it exciting. That's the focus: to make it as big and as wonderful and as thrilling as possible.' Director Martin Campbell explained that by combining explosive action, heart-stopping stunts and trademark humour, this seventeenth James Bond action adventure had all the elements to make it a worthy successor to the series. 'It is a mixture of tradition and invention.'

For the most part Brosnan appeared calm about the onerous legacy he had inherited. Some days he felt he had performed well. At other times, he questioned his approach. 'I have to make him real,' he repeated. As the advance publicity proclaimed: 'Bond is back – with a vengeance!', providing plenty of opportunity for those key, larger-than-life Bond-style stunts, which combine so magnificently with mind-boggling technical brilliance with amusing implausibility. Such set pieces are hallmarks, like the swish automobiles (in *GoldenEye* it is the sleek, stylish BMW Z3 Roadster seen before it became available to the general public, though the beloved Aston Martin DB5 also puts in an appearance); the 'shaken, not stirred': line and, of course, his own inimitable way with the ladies.

Devices and gadgets are another Bond trademark. The screen hero's faithful fans would have been watching for the tradition to be fully maintained in *GoldenEye*, and they would not be disappointed. *GoldenEye* introduced a new Bond armed with a seemingly ordinary ballpoint pen that becomes a deadly grenade with three clicks of the button, a watch with a built-in laser, and a leather belt with a buckle that fires 75 feet of high-tensile wire designed to hold 007's weight. Stretching credulity? Producer Michael Wilson said: 'Many of the gadgets we came up with are not that far removed from what will be developed in the near future. We tend to be just slightly ahead of reality, and as time passes, we begin to see the same idea becoming adopted in real life.'

GoldenEye (running time 130 minutes) was released in the United States on 13 November 1995, in London on 21 November and generally throughout Britain on 24 November. It was in London that the film's royal premiere took place, at the Odeon, Leicester Square, attended by Prince Charles. Pierce was there of course, accompanied by Keely Shaye-Smith, his new girlfriend, and members of his family, to receive a rapturous welcome from fans. He also attended the New York premiere with, this time, his mother May and Keely, again.

Winter is not generally the best time of the year for big-budget action films to be released, and opening in November did *GoldenEye* few favours. There were a few tense days, followed by rising hopes. Pierce, along with everyone else involved, watched the audience figures climb. The box office was beginning to look buoyant. Who dared to say 007 was in decline? As attendance figures continued to climb impressively, Brosnan must have felt that his £1.5 million fee for the picture had indeed been earned, that he had been good value for money.

GoldenEye went on to smash box-office records internationally, eventually grossing in excess of $350 million. It failed to exceed

Thunderball in terms of audience figures, but was well ahead of *Moonraker* (1979), which was, until *GoldenEye*, the highest-grossing Bond film in the series, at $203 million. Not only did the performance of *GoldenEye* fully vindicate the choice of Pierce Brosnan as the new 007, but showed that after more than thirty years and seventeen films, James Bond was still a powerful force in cinemas worldwide.

9

Top Billing

WHEN PIERCE BROSNAN WALKED OFF the film set at Leavesden at the end of shooting of *GoldenEye* in June 1995 he didn't celebrate, put his feet up or fly off on a long holiday. He felt pretty good. He was satisfied with his own performance and knew he could not have done more to uphold the special traditions of one of the screen's greatest ever characters. A celebration, certainly, would not have been out of order.

What was still a lottery at the time, however, was the worldwide public response to the return of James Bond, in the form of Pierce Brosnan as an updated 007 for the 1990s. In one sense it was an academic question for Brosnan. For it was not the world's best-kept secret that he had already signed a contract with Eon Productions that committed him to returning to play James Bond at least twice more. Indeed such was Eon's confidence that they had taken the crucial decision way back in May, with ten days of filming still left on *GoldenEye*, to press ahead as soon as possible with the next Bond epic, *Tomorrow Never Dies*. The record-breaking box office receipts from *GoldenEye* gave the new Bond project additional impetus.

Brosnan was naturally delighted with his success as James Bond, but was also concerned to do other movies and play different kinds of parts. He was determined to widen his experience.

111

It would mean a heavy schedule, but his ambition was strong. So between the worldwide release of *GoldenEye* during November and December 1995 and the start of shooting on *Tomorrow Never Dies* in April 1997 – around eighteen months at most – Brosnan would go before the cameras in three totally different movies. In two of them he appeared in supporting roles; in the third, a disaster thriller, he played the lead.

The Mirror Has Two Faces, shot mainly in New York during the winter of 1995/6, was a vehicle for the multi-talented Barbra Streisand. Described by more than one person as the most powerful woman in Hollywood Streisand, by her own admission, is not always easy to work with. She has strong views on how movies should be made and when she is in charge likes to be in complete control. Her critics claim her demands are often excessive, and her obsession with perfection unrealistic given the constraints of time and money. In *The Mirror Has Two Faces* she not only played the leading role, but also directed the movie and, along with Marvin Hamlisch, composed the background music. One of the less charitable reviewers was at pains to point out that '. . . she gets all the best lines too, rattling off satirical quips like an equine Woody Allen with breasts'. Another critic felt it important to point out that Streisand received in all no fewer than twelve separate credits in the picture including Music Supervision and Composer of Love Theme.

Streisand's presentation, based on a 1958 French film starring Michele Morgan, is a romantic comedy which tells the story of handsome college maths professor Gregory Larkin (Jeff Bridges) who, after becoming disillusioned with a string of rather dreary flings, decides that carnal intimacy only ruins relationships. So he goes in search of a less attractive woman with whom he can enjoy a more stable, platonic relationship; they could simply be friends, based on intellectual stimulation, without sex getting in the way. When, by a roundabout way, he finds her, a fellow professor called

Rose Morgan (a frumpy, bespectacled Streisand), all seems to be going well for a time – so well they even get married. Only then does he discover that Rose is not the sexually demure innocent he assumed. She was never in the market for sterile companionship; just the opposite in fact, as she now goes after him for love, sex and romance in a big way.

Streisand has never been Hollywood's favourite person and always needs to pluck something really special out of the hat to avoid the cliché-ridden, carping comments about her profile, her ego and her so-called megalomania. Frequent reports of Streisand tantrums on the set didn't help her reputation, nor was the sacking of Dudley Moore (George Segal taking over) shortly after the start of production, along with the walk-out of cinematographer Dante Spinotti, citing 'creative differences'. Certainly, *The Mirror Has Two Faces* was no *Yentl*; not even *A Star is Born*. But as a light, romantic comedy it wasn't all that bad either, if a trifle long at two hours. The story was by Richard LaGravenese, and while competent enough, never achieved the conviction or sensitivity of his *The Bridges of Madison County* which had been released the previous year. In fairness, however, it was a very different type of movie, first setting up, then demolishing, the theory that a marriage can survive without sex.

Streisand had assembled a competent and experienced cast headed by Jeff Bridges, son of Lloyd Bridges who made a number of movies in the 1940s and 1950s and was popular on television from 1958 to 1960, when he appeared as a favourite wet-suited underwater hero in the highly successful children's series, *Sea Hunt*. Jeff had already achieved much in a distinguished movie career spread over more than twenty years. He secured an Oscar nomination as Best Supporting Actor for a pivotal performance in only his second film, Peter Bogdanovich's poignant *The Last Picture Show*, in 1971. An undoubted box-office favourite over many years, Bridges never quite achieved the star rating it was felt should have been his, though he was consistently in work, appearing in more than twenty movies during the eighties and early nineties.

The remainder of the cast, in addition to George Segal, a movie veteran of more than forty films, included Mimi Rogers, the legendary Lauren Bacall and the model Elle Macpherson. So Brosnan was in respected company and performed ably enough in the limited opportunities afforded by, as one critic put it, his B-movie role. He also managed to dodge the flak which seemed to rain down on the set from time to time.

Brosnan's part as Streisand's character's brother-in-law was hardly substantial. He was not on screen anything like as often as his fans would have wanted, but he managed to side-step the tantrums of perfectionist Streisand. He simply said how much he admired her enormous talent and professionalism behind and in front of the cameras. 'She's a woman who knows what she wants,' he commented. 'She's a huge movie star, but a woman who is also very vulnerable.'

Playing the high-profile James Bond had given Brosnan a ready point of recognition with the public, so he was positioned well up the cast list immediately behind Streisand and Bridges. Despite his part being little more than a cameo, he widened his experience as an actor and gained prestige by working with some top-notch performers in what was essentially a Streisand vehicle. For Pierce it served the purpose of letting movie-goers see him in a totally different kind of role. For Streisand it provided the opportunity to develop her lungs as a movie-maker. A two-star rating seemed fair, but nobody, not even Streisand, ever contemplated Oscar nominations, though surprisingly perhaps, the film's theme tune, 'I've Finally Found Someone', did receive an Oscar nomination.

Unfortunately *The Mirror Has Two Faces* received a battering by the critics. *Total Film* called it an 'ugly duckling' of a tale and added: 'As a movie it's old-fashioned – comfortably chucklesome, but so predictable you can see the plot being hand-twisted.' And that was one of the better reviews! Typical among the comments was that the picture seemed rather dated and sedate, almost a throw-back to the Doris Day–Rock Hudson type of movie of yesteryear. Curiously the film fared much better at the hands of the reviewers when it became available on video some years later, one report picking out 'a smart script which was frequently quite brilliant . . . and an admirable Bacall which made for terrific viewing.'

When *Mars Attacks!* was released in Britain little more than a month later, British filmgoers had another early chance to see Pierce Brosnan, this time in a meatier role. Film-makers find their inspiration in all manner of weird and wonderful places and situations – from comments overheard in everyday life, from books and magazines, through travelling, thinking and from personal experiences of themselves and others. But from 'swap' cards given free with every pack of bubble gum? Seems odd, perhaps, but not when you understand that Tim Burton, the director of *Mars Attacks!*, is not the most conventional of movie directors. Yet few achieved the kind of success he enjoyed in the late 1980s.

Born and raised in Burbank, surrounded by Hollywood's film and television industry, Burton was none the less a timid, withdrawn child. But like Brosnan he had a talent for drawing and art, and after winning a scholarship to the California Institute of the Arts, he studied animation there. At Disney, where he began work, his bizarre imagination was soon found to be at odds with the company's philosophy and clean-cut image, but recognizing his special brand of talent and creativity, they decided to keep him on the payroll.

Several short animations he created while with Disney were acknowledged as being distinctive, like his award-winning six-minute dedication piece called *Vincent*, narrated by his childhood hero Vincent Price. It won a number of awards and was later released commercially. A live-action 29-minute feature called

Frankenweenie, about a boy who reanimates his dead dog, was considered unsuitable for release, but led to Burton securing his first feature directing assignment at the tender age of twenty-five on *Pee Wee's Big Adventure*, a slapstick fantasy released in 1985, which, according to Pauline Kael of the *New Yorker*, had the 'bouncing-along inventiveness of a good cartoon'.

But to return to those bubble-gum cards. They were a successful sales gimmick, which began in the United States, at first focusing on baseball stars. Next came a 55-card set called *Mars Attacks!* inspired by the gruesome imagery of sci-fi B-movies of the time. But their lurid graphics created such an outcry, mainly from parents anxious to protect their children, that they had to be withdrawn. They were later reintroduced, much toned down and based on an epic alien invasion of earth. Burton's fertile mind locked on to the idea, visualizing their possibilities in film terms.

Mars Attacks! was the result. Burton said at the time: 'You take something like that away from kids and they want it even more. That's where the whole dynamic came from, they became very cultish items. They are very mild by today's standards.' By the time *Mars Attacks!* went into production Burton was something of a power player in the movie business; his full-length feature, *Batman*, in 1989 pulled off a major surprise, becoming one of the highest-grossing movies in history. *Batman Returns*, a follow-up with Burton again directing, appeared in 1992.

For *Mars Attacks!*, a madcap spoof about an alien invasion of the earth, Burton did a remarkable job in attracting such a star-studded cast. The high-profile Jack Nicholson, who appeared in Burton's massively successful *Batman*, headed the list after Burton's abortive attempt to sign Warren Beatty. The director claimed: 'When I approached Nicholson to see if he would play a part he typically wisecracked: "Sure . . . I'll play 'em all!" I told him a couple would do!' Also in the line-up were Glenn Close, Pierce Brosnan of course, Annette Bening, Danny DeVito, Michael

J. Fox, Lukas Haas, Sarah Jessica Parker, Martin Short, Rod Steiger and Tom Jones.

With a $70 million budget, the picture was a surreal, sardonic satire populated by bulbous-eyed freaks intent on moving in on earth, cleverly interspersed with touches of keen humour. But the real triumph was surely the technology, the animations and the amazing digital special effects that made it all possible. These were provided by Industrial Light and Music, a specialist company with an impressive pedigree that included all the special effects and animations for *Jurassic Park*. Their work was guaranteed to make the greatest impact with audiences: Las Vegas in ruins; Flying Saucers atomizing conventional aircraft; the White House in panic; Congress blown up; and Martians running wild across the United States. With such an onslaught the plot, quite rightly, was secondary. It was a Burton extravaganza at its best: 'sickly hilarious' said one critic; another: 'If it wasn't the funniest thing on celluloid right now, you'd have to ban it!'

The film starts slowly, but once the Martians land on earth proclaiming they come in peace, why do we all get the feeling that it is only a matter of time before all hell breaks loose? Their real purpose is, of course, the earth's ultimate destruction. Little wonder one critic described it as being 'at the same time, horrifying and humorous'.

Much of the picture was filmed in New York City but Washington and Las Vegas featured strongly as locations. The sequences cleverly focus on various individuals in different locations as they struggle with their own dramas. Las Vegas is where we witness Tom Jones overdosing on his trademark song 'It's Not Unusual' just before the aliens strike and his gig is blown away. As the attack goes global, London, in particular Big Ben and the Houses of Parliament, becomes a target for the little men from outer space.

Nicholson gives his customary first-class performance in a

double role. First, he plays a self-serving US president who, in the words of one reviewer, is more worried about re-election than an attack from Mars; and he is also equally convincing as a sleazy Vegas real-estate tycoon adorned with 'fright wig and false teeth'. Glenn Close is the President's First Lady, Sarah Jessica Parker and Michael J. Fox are rival television reporters, Rod Steiger is a military general at odds with press secretary Martin Short, and Tom Jones plays himself, while (along with Bening and DeVito) preparing to do battle with the invaders. Brosnan is convincing as Donald Kessler, a pipe-smoking English scientist, alongside Bening, who plays his scatter-brained wife.

Kessler is a close aide to the President, but is slow to pick up on why the Martians have landed. It was, as Brosnan himself pointed out, a great opportunity for him to play against type, and he takes his chance skilfully. He even delivers one of the best lines in the entire film. As a trusting pacifist convinced there must be some logical and innocent explanation for the attack, he warns the President not to take the attack too seriously. With deadpan profundity, he suggests, 'It could just be a cultural misunderstanding.' All this, as death-rays are frying human flesh in a flash.

For his pains Pierce's character finally meets a fate worse than death itself. Not only does he have his head chopped off, but the decapitated head continues to be able to speak! When Burton said he saw *Mars Attacks!* as good fun, you could see what he meant.

Technically it was a work of genius, a fine example of Burton's unique imagination and ingenuity. 'It's a great "screamish" movie,' one dedicated fan enthused. But for an actor who had so recently been 'top of the bill' in a James Bond blockbuster and commercial record-breaking movie, both *The Mirror Has Two Faces* (released in the United States 1996 and Britain in January 1997) and *Mars Attacks!* (released around the same time) must have disappointed his rapidly growing number of fans. They saw too little of their hero in both films, which themselves fell well short as Brosnan

118

vehicles. Having shared the euphoria of Pierce's remarkable overnight leap to international stardom with *GoldenEye*, they were waiting impatiently for his next high-profile blockbuster.

The Mirror Has Two Faces and *Mars Attacks!* never had a chance of sustaining his reputation as the new golden boy of planet Hollywood. Both pictures were a little offbeat for popular taste and neither had film critics toppling off their chairs with excitement. Brosnan did not see it in those terms. For him it was the actor-versus-star dilemma again. He was making a conscious effort to broaden and deepen his experience as an actor. In this context top billing was not all-important. That would come again with the next James Bond movie. In any case, it all depended on what films were available, and what he was offered. Meanwhile, he was at least being seen by the cinema-going public, and he was quick to point out how important it was for him to be working with some of the top people in the business, as he had done in his last two movies.

With *Dante's Peak*, Brosnan's third movie to be released in Britain in 1997, he had certainly saved the best till last, in both commercial and artistic terms. This was going some considerable way towards what the fans wanted to see. The picture was directed by the highly respected Roger Donaldson, who had moved to New Zealand from his native Australia in 1965, where he set up a photographic business. This led to an apprenticeship in moving pictures, making television commercials and documentaries, and in 1977 he produced his first motion picture, *Sleeping Dogs*. A political drama set in the near future, it certainly had its faults, but it was also significant as New Zealand's first feature film in fifteen years, as well as the first from that country ever to be shown in American cinemas.

By the early 1980s Donaldson had gained enough of a reputation to attract the attention of Italian-born producer Dino De Laurentiis, who made no secret of his love of overblown film spectaculars. In 1984 De Laurentiis had salvaged the Mel Gibson–Anthony Hopkins movie *The Bounty* after it looked set to run aground, recruiting Donaldson to direct after a bitter disagreement between the original director David Lean and screenwriter Robert Bolt. The ensuing years saw Donaldson working with such Hollywood top-notchers as Costner and Cruise.

Dante's Peak was an all-action disaster-thriller from major studio Universal with an impressive $100 million budget, much of it spent on impressive state-of-the-art special effects. Filmed in just six hectic weeks, it was a substantial project and early studio gossip had tipped Michael Douglas for the lead role of Dr Harry Dalton. Dalton is a young widower, and a cool, serious volcano expert, who is asked to investigate minor seismic activity near the remote Dante's Peak, a small and idyllic community town of 8,000 people nestled at the foot of a towering mountain in the Northern Cascades in America's Pacific North-West.

Brosnan, who only a short time before had said that he saw himself more as a character actor than a leading man, was surprised and delighted to be chosen to top the cast list opposite Linda Hamilton. She was some four years younger than her co-star and had made her movie debut in 1982. Hollywood had, however, seemed surprisingly casual about how best to develop her potential, though she had appeared in the Arnold Schwarzenegger blockbuster *Terminator 2: Judgment Day*, which was the biggest box-office success of 1991.

Twister, released just a year before *Dante's Peak*, had unleashed the enormous potential of movies that focused on natural disasters. Generally hounded by critics with lines like 'Another theme-park ride of a movie . . .' and 'It's the world's first thriller about thin air . . .', it none the less grossed more than $493 million round the world. Brosnan was somewhat circumspect about his new picture, cautiously optimistic about its commercial possibilities, but obviously pleased with its pace and excitement. 'This is a heart-stopping film,' he said. 'It just pumps along from the very first frame to the end. There's no room to move, there's no room to breathe. Certainly the volcano is one of the main stars of the film, but the relationships between the characters have not been compromised as a result.'

Brosnan had grown up with *The Towering Inferno* and *The Poseidon Adventure*. 'I loved seeing mankind at its wits' end, up against a towering inferno or a sinking ship,' he once said. But he still had much to learn about natural disasters and embarked on an extensive programme of research to prepare for the role. 'When you get into it, it's a fascinating subject,' he said after talking with volcanologists, watching documentaries and spending time with members of the US Geological Survey. They told him of first-hand experiences that had gone disastrously wrong. Brosnan explained that a community of geologists lost two of their best people a few years before when they simply got too close. 'They thought they had done the correct thing, thought they were on safe ground, but a pyroclastic cloud came up and took them away.'

The subject obviously fascinated Brosnan. 'These people who do it, live for it,' he enthused. 'They wait for the big one to happen. God's big show.' He revealed something of the actor within himself, explaining that you read about it all, try to focus strongly and deeply on the enormity of such happenings. Then you use your imagination as an actor; you say, 'How would I react? And you put a lot of trust in your director and the people around you.'

Dante's Peak has a simple, but effective plot. When Brosnan's character, Harry Dalton, goes to investigate some minor rumblings at a volcano which, though dormant for years, now needs to be investigated urgently, he is shocked to find evidence that suggests a catastrophic eruption is imminent. Locals find it hard to accept that the benevolent, placid-looking mountain could be a threat to their well-being, their homes, their very existence. Nothing could happen to disturb their tranquil lifestyle. But the danger is real; a sleeping giant is awakening.

Dalton's shock at their reaction turns into disbelief and horror when he finds that the town authorities are keen to put a lid on his startling discovery. They ignore his frantic warnings, because they are close to pulling off a major business deal for the town that will substantially boost the local economy. If Dalton's news leaks out negotiations will collapse and the deal will be lost. Dalton also has serious trouble trying to convince his own boss of the looming danger.

Linda Hamilton plays Rachel Wando, a single mother with two young children, son Graham (Jeremy Foley) and daughter Lauren (Jamie Renee Smith), to look after and think about; she is also the town's mayor. She finally heeds the warning and calls an emergency meeting; but it's all a bit late. At a tense moment the volcano seizes the initiative and the attention of every member of the audience as it explodes into life . . . vivid, cruel and with a force, as advance publicity informed, equal to the power of a million atomic bombs. Brosnan is shown heroically fleeing the river of lava, along with scores of panic-stricken townspeople. As one review put it: 'The film takes audiences on a terrifying journey of mayhem and annihilation.'

Donaldson tackled his subject with courage and understanding, plus a high degree of realism, helped by specially constructed models, computer-generated graphics and, it seemed, unlimited tons of fake volcanic ash. Digital Domain pulled out all the stops with an impressive repertoire of special visual effects and digital animation. Thrown together in such dire circumstances it is hardly surprising that Brosnan and Hamilton find romance together. More than one report, however, suggested that the off-set relationship between the two stars was decidedly uncongenial.

'It was a thrill for me to be part of *Dante's Peak*,' explained Brosnan as the final scenes were being shot. He seemed intrigued by the way the human spirit survives extraordinary odds and was absorbed by being part of what he called a 'big event movie'. But although it was all make-believe, risks do have to be taken sometimes by actors intent on making a good and convincing movie. He recalled a scene where he and Hamilton, together with her two children and mother-in-law, are attempting to cross a river that has been turned to acid by the volcano's gases. 'The bloody boat sank,' he told *Film Review*. 'The bow went down and nine-year-old Jamie Renee (who plays Lauren in the film) couldn't swim. The propeller was still going, so we had to keep away from the boat. Then I realized the water wasn't all that deep. But it was scary for a moment, seeing little Jamie bob up and down.'

Back in the make-believe world, the children's grandmother is a victim of the disaster, but the children and their mother, along with the family dog, are all saved by Brosnan. He also survives after suffering a horrendous experience which leaves the audience breathless. The film was a formidable challenge to make, with no fewer than fifty-five names appearing on the list of 'stunt' credits.

GoldenEye apart, *Dante's Peak* was certainly the most important and impressive movie in the career of Pierce Brosnan up to that time. He had now been making movies professionally for more than fifteen years, and his selection as the new James Bond had given him saturation-level media coverage at an international level. Astonishing then to consider that *Dante's Peak* was the first big-budget Hollywood-made movie of his career – it brought what was almost certainly his biggest-ever pay packet, estimated by one source to be in excess of $7 million. Donaldson explained that in Brosnan he had found someone with international appeal, a sensitive actor and someone who was relatively new and obviously going places. Brosnan said he was pleased to do it, because it was a type of role he had never played before, giving him the chance to play against type. He did not want to be known for Bond alone.

The picture was filmed between June and October 1996 in

Idaho and in and around Los Angeles, the latter not far from home for Brosnan. As usual the schedules were tight and became further compressed when news filtered through that a competing disaster movie called *Volcano* was being speeded up in an effort to hit the cinemas ahead of *Dante's Peak*. Universal responded by bringing forward the release date of their film. It all became a little silly as the 'opposition' then advanced their release date even further; but where money is concerned – and the first picture out to the public, given encouraging reviews, could certainly steal the initiative – such tactical issues are important and have to be taken seriously.

On this occasion the Brosnan epic was first past the post, Universal having brought forward the picture's release in the all-important American market to 7 February 1997, a full month ahead of the original schedule. There was even a junior novelization from Puffin Books, available as the film was released.

Granted that in *The Mirror Has Two Faces* and *Mars Attacks!* Brosnan's time on screen was by no means excessive, having three films released in the space of just twelve months was a significant achievement, especially taking into account the tough mental and physical demands of Brosnan's leading role in *Dante's Peak*.

He had also managed somehow to sandwich this heavy schedule between the end of shooting *GoldenEye* and his second 007 movie, *Tomorrow Never Dies*, which began filming on 1 April 1997, just three days after *Dante's Peak* was released in Britain.

Brosnan was already discovering that Bond was all-demanding; but he was also aware that not one previous 007 – Connery, Moore, Dalton even – had managed to achieve a major box-office success outside the series during his reign as James Bond. Maybe finding the energy, time, desire, opportunity or resolve was the reason they appeared to be shackled to 007.

He would see that as something which he needed to avoid in his own career. He loved playing James Bond. It had been the pinnacle of his ambition as he struggled to make his name and to negotiate the difficult divide that separates television from the movies. But he was also determined not to be typecast, even in what was probably the most coveted role in movies. He would come to enjoy being a star, but he was determined to be known as an actor as well.

10
Life Goes On

IT SEEMED LIKE AN ORDINARY, routine sort of day for Keely Shaye-Smith – that is, if any day for an environmental journalist working for ABC television could be classed as such. She was in Mexico, far from her Los Angeles home, on a special assignment for the *Entertainment Tonight* programme. Then it happened. The man was reading a book. She asked him a question. He said afterwards: 'She was lovely. We hit it off immediately.'

The man was Pierce Brosnan. There was little doubt that the eco-journalist who appeared on *Good Morning America* and the new James Bond had more in common than an interest in his latest film; they also shared a concern about the preservation of the planet itself and, it appears, an instant, powerful interest in each other.

The encounter with Keely, late on in 1994, was as casual as that – some three years after Cassandra's tragic death. Since then it is hardly surprising that the tall, handsome and athletic Brosnan, with dark hair and blue eyes, had not been short of serious pursuers in the intervening years. But this meeting with Keely, he knew from the start, was different, very different.

He continued to mourn Cassie. But with the passing of time he had been able to focus more positively on what he called the

127

wonderful, adventurous years they had enjoyed together. The big regret was that she did not live to see him fulfil their shared ambition of his becoming the new James Bond and his widely acknowledged success in other, perhaps more varied and testing roles as an actor on the big-screen.

The memories of Cassie were always there, never more strongly than in the close unity he enjoyed with Charlotte, Christopher and Sean. They remained very much a family, even as the three of them began to emerge from childhood to gather together individual lives of their own. And in time Brosnan too began to look towards living again. 'Life has to go on,' he would say. 'You cannot live in the past forever.' And what was more natural than that the young widower should spend some of his time meeting and mixing with women.

But meeting Keely Shaye-Smith somehow felt special from the start. When they realized they were comparatively near neighbours in Malibu, it seemed right and natural that they should continue to see one another as often as possible. Not that Pierce by this time had any need to be short of female company.

In and around Hollywood, and indeed elsewhere, he had been clearly targeted as a wealthy widower and, still very much in the prime of life (he was just forty-one when he met Keely), a highly eligible prospect. The attention was flattering and Pierce made no secret of it. Reports of various liaisons began to appear in the press. His links with a well-known model, a television reporter, the former wife of rock star Bruce Springsteen and the widow of the singer Roy Orbison were all well enough documented. The media's interest was persistent. Photographers were out in force again when he and tennis champion Monica Seles attended a Los Angeles function together.

Pierce would sometimes, but by no means always, introduce the girl he was with to his family. Some relationships were more serious than others, but it is doubtful if any escaped media attention.

His links with Barbara Orbison, who had been a close friend of Cassie's, particularly during the dark days of her illness, and indeed of the family, were said to have been innocent enough before developing into a romance. Her singing star husband had died suddenly of a heart attack a couple of years before, and it is not surprising that their shared sense of loss should bring them closer together.

A reportedly wild fling which came to light some years later allegedly took place when Pierce was working on location in Yugoslavia for the television film *Death Train*. Attending church at Ljubljana, in Slovenia, he was said to have met Mateja Span, a young, dark-haired local beauty. According to her, the mutual attraction was instant. She said that within days their friendship had developed into something more. Once filming was over, the two of them reportedly travelled to Venice, where they spent some time together. Mateja claimed she had written about all this in her private diary. Before leaving, Brosnan was said to have given her a love poem, which he had composed specially for her.

When Pierce returned a couple of years later to shoot *Night Watch*, the sequel to *Death Train*, it seemed that whatever the relationship had been, it was not rekindled. Life had moved on. Even at the height of the reported liaison, not everything was as perfect as it appeared. Mateja said that she could tell he was troubled; his thoughts kept drifting back to Cassandra and the children.

But his new relationship with Keely Shaye-Smith seemed serious and sincere from the start. He certainly wanted it to develop, but at first he was tentative, anxious not to let things advance too quickly. Not until 1996, more than two years after their first meeting, did she move in with him. Even then she reportedly kept her own house going. But undoubtedly the relationship was developing in depth and security; years later, however, Brosnan would say that she was always an independent lady with her own career. But there was now a growing and satisfying stability in Pierce's life, which he hadn't known for a long time. And, it seems, genuine love.

At a professional level film work was now keeping Brosnan fully committed. Once the final scenes for *Dante's Peak* had been completed, he was thrust into a hectic programme of personal appearances and promotional activity. He had enjoyed making the picture and felt it had turned out well. The public, certainly in North America, largely shared his view and box office returns there would eventually exceed $60 million, but in Britain the response was more muted. The critics were almost collectively against it, with *Empire* hurling its most destructive salvos against 'the appalling dialogue' and, in particular, the way Brosnan delivered the line '. . . making love is like riding a bicycle – you never forget.' Despite generally disappointing reviews *Dante's Peak* went on to achieve worldwide sales of some $150 million, but with only a fraction of that coming in through the British box office.

A busy work schedule gave Brosnan little time to relax, and shortly after clearing away the remnants of *Dante's Peak* he headed out to Ireland to begin work on his next film. *The Nephew* was a meagre offering compared with James Bond, or *Dante's Peak* even, but still of significant personal interest and importance to Brosnan. For some time Pierce had nurtured a vision of creating his own movies and had recently taken the first step by establishing, along with his business partner and film producer friend, Beau St Clair, his own production company, named Irish Dream Time.

It is difficult to be precise about Brosnan's motives for setting up the company. He probably wanted to make some slightly less mainstream movies which tackled issues more deeply. He was certainly not the first Hollywood star to form his own company to make the kind of movies he wanted to make. Notable others included Kevin Costner and Clint Eastwood. Could it be also that he was beginning to plan for a time when he would not be the automatic choice for the James Bond role, a time when he didn't really want it anyway? After all, Connery had been forty-six when he last played the part, though Moore was considerably older when he threw in the towel, a youthful looking fifty-seven.

Brosnan explained at the time: 'I love Ireland. There are many people there that I grew up with and I loved going back there to make *The Nephew*.' He went on to say that the country has a sophisticated infrastructure for film-making. He talked about his hopes that Irish Dream Time would be able to become involved with bigger projects, and he specifically mentioned a remake of *The Thomas Crown Affair*, probably the first-ever hint of this ambitious, future project.

The Nephew was tiny by comparison. It tells the story of a farmer living on the small, remote (and fictional) island of Inis Daro off the coast of Ireland. He receives a letter telling him that his sister, whom he didn't get along with anyway, has died in the United States. He also learns that he has a nephew. When he goes to the ferry to meet his nephew he is not only surprised to find a seventeen-year-old African–American stepping up to greet him, but shocked to find that the boy is carrying his dead mother's ashes under his arm.

The boy finds his uncle, the only relation he has in the world, to be taciturn and reclusive, but he meets a young girl whose father owns the biggest pub on the island. As Brosnan put it: 'It's a very simple story about a young boy coming to terms with his loss; and the uncle coming to terms with his loss also. It's a story of secrets, grudges and lies. Most of the characters in *The Nephew* are complex, fractured people.'

The heart-warming tale revolves around relationships, rivalry and regrets and the unfolding of twenty years of family secrets. The well-respected farmer Tony Egan is played by Donal McCann, who would sadly die in July 1999 when only fifty-six; the role of his nephew, Chad, was taken by Hill Harper. Brosnan played Joe Brady, the bar owner who is at the centre of a long-standing feud.

His role is pivotal, but he by no means hogs the limelight: 'I saw it as an ensemble piece that showed off the talents of all those involved.' Sinead Cusack, a member of a well-established acting family well-known through British television, also featured in the film.

Making *The Nephew* so soon after *Dante's Peak* came as a severe culture shock for Brosnan. The latter film had the luxury of a budget in excess of $100 million. *The Nephew* had to scrape by on just $5 million. Mind you, it says much for Brosnan's personal reputation and influence that he was able to persuade United Artists to give him a production deal of any sort; to impress investors enough to stump up that amount of backing for a film like *The Nephew* was a triumph of sorts.

Pierce was forced to make other major adjustments while in Ireland. As the acknowledged star of *Dante's Peak* he had been accorded all the considerations, facilities and support services one could imagine, including a massive luxury motor-home as head-quarters; and money was no object. To come from there to what Brosnan described as 'being in the bogs of Ireland, in a tin can with lavatories that are overflowing and your backside freezing' is certainly a humbling experience, particularly for a superstar who had already been described as 'that effortlessly stylish Irishman'. 'But I loved it,' he said. 'It keeps you grounded and it's great fun to do.'

Brosnan not only played the part of the young girl's father, but was also the film's producer. That was another new challenge to overcome, for he was inexperienced in his new role and the weather didn't help. 'I was in Ireland with the rain coming side-ways at me, looking at a call sheet like I'd never looked at one before, because at the top it stated clearly: "Pierce Brosnan – Producer",' he said. 'And I was standing there thinking, "I'm a producer. It's raining! What do I do now"?'

He found that adding the producer byline to the credits was

considerably more than a formality, as many people seem to think. The pressure was intense and unrelenting, not to mention the ever-present weight of responsibility. 'You want the film to be rewarding for everyone involved, because you're the one who set the wheels in motion.' He likened it to parenting. 'You're dealing with people's egos and talents, and trying to foresee problems,' he explained.

The Nephew was shown exclusively on Sky Movies in two screenings in December 1998. The satellite channel had snapped it up while the major film outlets were trying to make up their minds about its commercial possibilities. The latter felt that in competition with the big blockbusters, a film like *The Nephew*, which had virtually no action and depended almost wholly on a strong storyline and characterization for its success, was risky. Apparently Universal International Pictures was all set to distribute the movie in Britain when BSkyB came along and bought it from them for a figure that, it was said, the studio could not refuse. It was therefore not shown in cinemas around the country, though it became something of a box-office favourite when shown in some cinemas across Ireland. Brosnan seemed pragmatic about all this. 'It's hard when you're up against the big-budget films to get noticed,' he explained. He told *Sky Magazine*: 'I wanted to do a small movie about something that was intimate and had a strong storyline. I think this film has a good heart.'

Brosnan was much more than just the producer of *The Nephew*. He had been closely involved with almost every facet of the movie right from the beginning. 'It started from the script landing on my desk to meeting the director [Eugene Brady] and putting the crew together,' he explained. After the final scenes of the picture had been shot and all the ends tied up, it was his responsibility to put the picture to bed, before doing his share of promotion and publicity, taking up interview opportunities and personal appearances.

The Nephew was a courageous venture and Pierce never

expected it to be wildly successful commercially. After all it isn't the kind of movie you make if your over-riding objective is to make money. What was probably more depressing at the time was the long delay before the public had an opportunity to see it. It wasn't seen in Britain until 12 December 1998. Because it was being shown exclusively on Sky Movies, many thousands of people who might have enjoyed it therefore simply did not have the chance to see it.

Meanwhile Brosnan's personal life had been eventful. Back in June 1996 came the announcement that the 33-year-old Keely was pregnant, and on 13 January 1997, in what Pierce would call a magical moment, she gave birth to a son weighing nine pounds at the Cedars-Sinai Hospital in Los Angeles. He was delivered by caesarean section. Keely had been in labour for eight hours. The baby would be named Dylan Thomas. Pierce explained that he and Keely had decided that if the baby was a boy he would be called Dylan, a name they both liked very much. The second name was not difficult to choose either, since Pierce's father and Keely's father had both been christened Thomas . . . hence Dylan Thomas. Pierce had driven Keely to the hospital and was there at the birth. The whole family was said to be delighted.

Less than three months later, Pierce as a proud father for the second time, but now with four children to look after, was reporting for duty on his next Bond assignment, *Tomorrow Never Dies*. On 17 July 1997, a scene was being shot for the fifth time when a stunt man's metal helmet caught him awkwardly in the face, close to the mouth. It happened so quickly that hardly anyone saw the incident, but it caused anxiety, for the wound, though little more than an inch and a half long, had cut into the flesh deeply. Close-ups seemed to be at risk. At first Brosnan did not realize anything was wrong. But after the studio nurse arrived on set, as a precaution Pierce was driven over to Mount Vernon Hospital in Northwood, Middlesex, which specializes in plastic surgery.

Timing now became a serious problem because the film-makers were already battling hard to achieve the film's scheduled December release. If hold-ups from the accident were to put back the schedule, even for a week, thousands of pounds would be added to the budget. Fortunately it turned out that the injury could have been much worse. Incredibly *Tomorrow Never Dies* was released as scheduled, appearing nationwide in Britain on 12 December 1997 – exactly a year to the month earlier than *The Nephew* was first shown on BSkyB.

As Brosnan made preparations for the rigours of his second outing as James Bond, he would have reflected on one significant change. For the one man who, more than anyone else in the world, had transformed Fleming's famous fictional character into a movie icon was not around anymore.

Albert R. 'Cubby' Broccoli, whose severe illness had kept him off the set during the making of *GoldenEye*, had died. His death at the age of eighty-seven, in June 1996, had punched a gaping hole in the creative powerhouse behind James Bond. It was him, along with his early partner Harry Saltzman, who first identified the potential of James Bond in film terms; and he had the vision, courage, foresight and determination to transform Bond into the most popular film franchise of all time.

Films generally, and in later years James Bond films specifically, were Broccoli's life. His illustrious career spanned five decades. He had started in the business at the bottom, as the humble assistant who called reveille for the Native American extras in *The Outlaw*, the half-baked Western which caused such a stir when the busty Jane Russell comforted a feverish Jack Beutel by actually getting into bed with him. But that was way back in 1943!

Broccoli was a native of Long Island, New York, but became a major contributor to the British film industry, producing over thirty international movies in this country. In 1987 he received the OBE (Order of the British Empire) and was also named

PIERCE BROSNAN

Commandeur des Arts et des Lettres by the French government.
Five years earlier he had received the coveted Irving G. Thalbert
Award in recognition of his outstanding achievements as a
producer of motion pictures.

It was in the 1950s that he first had the idea of bringing James
Bond to the screen, when he was in partnership with Irving Allen
in a business called Warwick Films, but his vision never material-
ized. Meantime Harry Saltzman had secured an option on the
screen rights to the James Bond novels, but it was only after Cubby
had formed Eon Productions with Saltzman that the Bond idea
began to look promising.

At first the obstacles had seemed insurmountable and the objec-
tions difficult to counter. Nobody could deny the prodigious
worldwide impact Fleming's books had made by 1961. The major
film studios, however, persisted in being unimpressed about 007's
big-screen potential. They claimed he was too British and that the
stories were too blatantly sexual. Then in 1962 came the breakthrough. After a conversation lasting just forty-five minutes with
the then head of United Artists, Arthur Krim, the studio agreed to
back the film adaptation of Ian Fleming's *Dr No* with a budget of
$1 million. The hope was that it would become the first film in a
modestly successful series. For Broccoli it was the realization of
one of his greatest ambitions.

He made *Dr No* and in October 1962 brought the fictional
James Bond to the movie screen for the first time. Six years later
Broccoli was able to bring *Chitty Chitty Bang Bang*, another
famous Ian Fleming story, this time for children, into the movies;
but the future for Albert R. Broccoli was destined to rest with
James Bond. In eight 007 films released between 1962 and 1974
Broccoli shared the producer credits with Saltzman, but when the
latter moved on to other projects, Broccoli took over exclusively
for *Moonraker*, *For Your Eyes Only*, *Octopussy*, *A View to a Kill*
and *The Living Daylights*, before sharing producer credits again,

136

but this time with Michael G. Wilson for *Licence To Kill*.

While he had not produced *GoldenEye*, the only film in which Brosnan had so far featured as Bond, his influence was manifest. 'He was ailing terribly during the making of *GoldenEye*,' said Brosnan. 'There will always be a place there that he occupied.' And so the memory, the emotion, the unseen presence of Cubby Broccoli was felt by cast and crew, and not least by Pierce Brosnan himself, as they gathered to bring to life the latest exploits of agent 007. The legacy of Bond lived on.

11

For Bond, Read Brosnan

WHEN THE EIGHTEENTH JAMES BOND MOVIE, *Tomorrow Never Dies*, opened for public viewing in Britain on 9 December 1997, our film hero was thirty-five years old. Yet he had already died four times!

The first death came in infancy, not long after his birth, when Sean Connery appeared in the guise of James in the opening movie, *Dr No*. The picture was a big hit, grossing $60 million way back in 1962. Everybody applauded what was a wonderful achievement. But the cynics soon had it killed off. A marvellous one-off, they conceded, but surely not the sort of thing you can do again. Yet when Connery, as Bond, got together with Bernard Lee as M, Louis Maxwell as Miss Moneypenny and the remainder of the Bond gang just a year later to make *From Russia With Love*, the box office grossed a remarkable $79 million. So James sallied forth.

The second death was reported on 12 August 1964, when author Ian Lancaster Fleming, creator of James Bond in his book *Casino Royale*, published in 1953, died of a heart attack, aged fifty-six. *The Times* even ran an obituary for James Bond. By this time, however, *Goldfinger* had already been made and was released in Britain the very next month (17 September 1964). But surely, with the creator of the character now departed, it must be time for James to hang up all his gadgets, send his women packing and quietly disappear from the scene. But *Goldfinger* would gross a record $125 million.

In 1977 poor old Bond would die for a third time. Ian Fleming wrote twelve full-length James Bond novels. *The Man with the Golden Gun* was published in 1965 and turned into a Bond movie for release in time for Christmas 1974. By this time all Fleming's books about James Bond had been made into films, so surely, no more stories meant no more films, especially since box office returns had dropped to a disappointing $98 million. By this time Bond was looking more like Roger Moore.

The undertakers came out for a fourth time when Pierce Brosnan was cast as Bond and *GoldenEye* was being made ready for production. James had once been a Cold War warrior, but was now a sad, politically correct bore – so kill him off. James had now been out-Bonded, so to speak, by the dynamic Bruce Willis and Arnold Schwarzenegger, not to mention the *Lethal Weapons* of Mel Gibson. James's previous effort in *Licence to Kill* could only pull in $156 million at the box office, the lowest return for seven years – so gun him down now with his own Walther PPK. But as Andrew Collins in the *Observer* once pointed out: 'Reports of James Bond's demise are always greatly exaggerated.' How true, and this time it was left to Pierce Brosnan to resuscitate Bond with his triumphant reincarnation in *GoldenEye*, which took a sizzling $350 million from the box office in 1995.

So Pierce had much to live up to when he reported for work on *Tomorrow Never Dies*. Of course, he was already committed to this his second Bond movie. His contract required it. But he was quite ready and more than willing to return to the world of 007. He did not feel in danger of being trapped by the character. 'I've done four pictures since *GoldenEye*, one of which I have produced, so I don't feel cornered at all,' he explained. 'This is just a wonderful thing to have in your back pocket.'

He did however voice some personal doubts about the world's master spy, though he may well have been bolstered by the results of an American television phone-in on the ideal choice for the next Bond. Brosnan came out top with an 85 per cent share of the vote. Even so, Brosnan had one or two niggling misgivings, despite Bond's enormous international success. 'It bothered me a bit that some of the James Bond essentials seemed to have become obscured in *GoldenEye*,' he revealed. He felt that some of the action sequences became sluggish at times and that James seemed to be losing a bit of his traditional touch with women. Brosnan had also been extremely nervous when shooting began on his baptism as Bond. But with that experience successfully under his belt, he felt more confident and relaxed when shooting started on *Tomorrow Never Dies* on 1 April 1997. . . .

. . . Or he might well have done had he not arrived for work on the early side of 8 a.m., looking pale, coughing badly and nursing a high temperature. It was April Fools' Day, the day immediately following the Easter break, and he had recently spent a few heavily committed weeks promoting *Dante's Peak*. It was certainly not the best time to be succumbing to a bout of flu. Co-producer Barbara Broccoli later admitted that beyond all the worries and responsibilities that mount up at the start of a new picture, her biggest concern at the start of that first day of work was her major star. 'He sounds awful. He's a total pro, but this is not the best way to launch a picture,' she explained anxiously.

The timescale for the new movie, working back from its scheduled release in early December 1997 to capture the all-important Christmas trade in Britain and the United States, meant that the film-makers had less time to complete *Tomorrow Never Dies* than for any previous Bond movie. Performing as Bond is a mammoth undertaking for any actor, and this latest adventure would be far more expensive, time-consuming and complicated to pull together than any of its predecessors. But that important early decision to go ahead with *Tomorrow Never Dies* had at least enabled American writer Bruce Feirstein to move off to a flying start on the screenplay. Yet the nature of the creative process meant that seemingly endless changes, new ideas, adjustments and rewrites would have to be hastily absorbed perilously close to specified deadlines.

An early idea had been to develop a story linked in some way to Britain's handover of Hong Kong to the Chinese in the summer of 1997. It was topical enough, perhaps too topical, and the idea was eventually abandoned because it was felt that the historic event, though it was to take place only five months prior to the scheduled release of the picture, would be 'over and done with' in the public eye. In the end there was widespread consensus that this latest Bond adventure benefited from having a more dramatic script than its predecessors and incorporating more impressive locations.

Tomorrow Never Dies became the best and most spectacular of all the Bonds to that time with actors and film units using thirty locations, not only in Britain, but at such international destinations as exotic Bangkok in Thailand, Tijuana in Mexico and Biarritz, Tarbe and the Pyrenees in France, Hamburg in Germany and Arizona and Florida in the States. Twenty separate locations were used in Britain, from RAF airbases at Mildenhall and Lakenheath in Suffolk; the Naval Dockyard at Portsmouth; the *Financial Times* building in London; the Stoke Poges golf club in Buckinghamshire (where the ballroom would be transformed into 007's Hamburg hotel room in which he first encounters a former girlfriend, Paris Carver); a private home in Aylesbury; Fareham in Hampshire; the IBM headquarters near Heathrow Airport and Brent Cross shopping complex in north London. Such was the size of the operation that the full-time crew grew to well in excess of 700 at one point. The film would take twenty-three weeks of hectic activity to shoot with five separate units, working at various locations around the world. Shooting would often continue round the clock.

Britain, specifically Hertfordshire, would again be the operational headquarters, yet only after an astonishing set of circumstances reminiscent of the struggle for studio space during *GoldenEye*. A return to the former airfield and Rolls-Royce factory at Leavesden, which Eon Productions had impressively converted into film-making studios for the previous Bond, seemed to be the obvious and sensible option. But in the meantime these facilities, which had been bought by a Malaysian consortium and renamed Millennium Studios, were already booked up for pre-production work on the new Star Wars movie, leaving insufficient space available to accommodate another blockbuster. Second choice Pinewood Studios did not have enough available capacity to handle the entire production, but in the end certain scenes would be shot there.

This was a serious setback so early in the project, and the possibility of filming the entire picture overseas was even fleetingly considered. In the end Eon Productions had little choice but to construct their own facilities, as before. But where? The search eventually hit on a former supermarket warehouse that was standing empty in the small Hertfordshire town of Frogmore, close to historic St Albans. It was well situated within easy reach of London and immediately available. With time running out, an almost manic conversion schedule – just eight weeks to completion – was undertaken.

At a cost of £2 million, the work would include the building of three sound stages and all the service and support facilities, such as dressing rooms, space for wardrobe and make-up departments, toilets, showers, even a small gymnasium. As soon as the conversion was over, the film-makers hurried in and production got started. Much of the picture would be shot at Frogmore, which in the end had to cope with representing six separate major locations.

At the same time studio gossip had it that difficulties were being encountered in casting the all-important villain. Eon Productions made reassuring noises suggesting all was under control, but it was later revealed that unsuccessful approaches had been made to Terence Stamp, Anthony Hopkins and even Sean Connery (that really would have been confusing), before a final decision was confirmed. In truth it had been a close call. On the first day of filming casting director Debbie McWilliams had still to secure confirmation of Jonathan Pryce as villain Elliot Carver; and negotiations were apparently still going on with MGM to secure Teri Hatcher.

Joint-producers of *Tomorrow Never Dies* were Michael G. Wilson and Barbara Broccoli, and the film was directed by Roger Spottiswoode. Roger was brought in after Martin Campbell, who had directed *GoldenEye* so successfully, declined, because he preferred not to do two consecutive Bond movies. Though Canadian by birth Spottiswoode had been raised in Britain and had graduated to feature films after editing television advertisements and documentaries before moving to Hollywood. He made his directorial debut with *Terror Train*, with Jamie Lee Curtis, in 1980, and gained widespread acclaim with the political drama *Under Fire* in 1983. In 1990 he had directed the all-action Mel Gibson feature *Air America*. Spottiswoode then gained widespread public attention with the highly-charged movie *And The Band Played On*, in 1993, a powerful dramatization of Randy Shilts' book about the early years of AIDS.

But directing Bond was surely his biggest challenge to date. And his comments gave more than a hint of the responsibility he felt. 'Bond is such an institution that everyone you know gives you ideas, but you have to be careful. One would not like to be known as the guy who ends the series.'

Making a James Bond movie is a full-time job, as Brosnan had discovered when making *GoldenEye*. The demands of *Tomorrow Never Dies* were anticipated to be even greater, and he might well have felt that he started earning his reputed $3 million fee well ahead of his first call on set. Having moved into a comfortable rented house near Hampstead Heath in north London, Brosnan was left with little leisure time there as the film, and the tempo of his life, built up momentum. As with *GoldenEye*, twelve- to four-teen-hour working days on the set were not uncommon, and Pierce's routine would often begin at dawn in Hampstead, followed all too soon by the arrival of the studio car, which would take him to Frogmore. There was little time to think about anything other than making the movie. Running through those important lines and tricky scenes in one's head would often be fitted in while travelling to the studio and during any other convenient moments snatched during a full and often heavily committed working day. Location work, both in Britain and overseas, would shatter routine and often add to the residual pressures.

To enable Pierce to cope better with the purely physical demands of the new picture, a small gymnasium was set up in his house and a personal trainer, Richard Smedley, appointed. In the beginning, particularly, Pierce's day could start in the early hours with an energetic run of five or six miles across Hampstead Heath. This was part of a carefully balanced programme to increase his physical stamina, maintain flexibility and sharpen his fitness levels. The dedicated routine also included regular weight-training work-outs. Pierce was a few pounds heavier than he had been for *GoldenEye*, and this, according to Smedley, a former soldier with the Parachute Regiment, was all to the good. 'The aim was for Pierce to have a strong look, since there were scenes in which it was important for him to show a good physique.' Those extra few pounds, along with the weight training, would do the trick. Diet was important too, and for the time being anyway, Brosnan's intake was by no means exotic or sophisticated enough to satisfy James Bond. Pierce's failing was allegedly his appetite for Kit-Kat bars. To make this kind of routine work, he had to make sure that his days were well disciplined.

Brosnan relished playing Bond a second time, having had critical acclaim for his debut as Bond two years before. 'The success of *GoldenEye* gave me new confidence,' he said. 'Last time it was a matter of getting my head down and delivering after a six-year delay.' He was delighted with the subtle changes that had been made in both the character of Bond and in the overall delivery of the film. He spoke with polite candour when he said that he felt earlier Bond movies hadn't been quite experimental enough. 'I was a little concerned that the new film would stick too closely to formula,' he confessed. 'But my fears were unfounded. Roger [Spottiswoode] brings a new vision to the series and he aims at more realism. There is moodier lighting and more realistic sets. And the action hero has changed since the time when Connery played Bond, and the new film reflects that. . . .

'I certainly felt we needed a bigger story this time around, and in truth it has never been bigger than in this latest movie. It is not only bigger, but bolder and better.' He found the fact that Bond had survived eighteen large-scale movies little short of miraculous. 'Can you imagine eighteen Lethal Weapons or eighteen Batmans?' A minor miracle indeed – it was estimated that more than two billion people had seen a James Bond film at the cinema, equivalent then to almost half of the entire population of the world. He went on: 'The joy of Bond is that he can change, adapt and be updated. He will now be pulling in new, first-time audiences in exactly the same way that he did in the early Sixties. That's not down to me, but the team of producers and writers who have kept him going.'

Brosnan's calm professionalism was evident and on the set he was said to be popular with and accessible to the crew. Those close to the action noticed a new assurance in Brosnan's approach to the business of Bond, second time around. He seemed even more impressive than in *GoldenEye*. 'The part is mine, the shoes fit,' was his succinct account of his inner sense of security.

He gave credit to actors like Mel Gibson and Harrison Ford, whose film heroes he said had not merely been fiercely masculine, but had also had charm, vulnerability and accessibility. 'So today you can look behind the curtain of Bond a little bit and see what makes him tick. You have to make him as real as possible within his fantasy world.' The astute co-producer Michael G. Wilson had plenty of opportunity to observe Brosnan in action at close hand during the filming of *Tomorrow Never Dies*. He said he was positive, mature and deliberate. 'He has the ability to draw the audience into the film through the eyes of the character,' he said.

With an estimated budget approaching $100 million, filming the then currently most expensive Bond film of all time was a relentless marathon that consumed furious thought and activity for almost eight uninterrupted months. Said Brosnan: 'There was a constant race against time to get *Tomorrow Never Dies* on screen.' The first scenes, for the pre-title sequence, were shot high up in the French Pyrenees in late January 1997, with the final work being handled on the huge 007 stage at Pinewood Studios in Buckinghamshire in early September. It was a relentless schedule and not everything turned out as planned. A potential crisis emerged within days of shooting when unexpectedly rising temperatures in the French Pyrenees transformed what should have looked like a remote mountain range in snowy Afghanistan into a useless quagmire. Hundred of locals had responded to an advertisement wanting to be part of a sequence, packed with special effects, that features an Afghan military base being blown up by the Russians. The Pyrenees would also double for the famous Khyber Pass in Afghanistan.

Another even more heart-pounding crisis occurred early on and nearer to home. The second film unit, in possession of all the permissions and authorizations required in order to shoot some important scenes in Vietnam, were almost en route to the airport when all the clearances were withdrawn. After some swift rejigging

147

and panicked activity, the location was switched to Thailand. A Vietnamese street was constructed at the Frogmore studios, but other shots purporting to be the streets of Saigon were actually filmed in Bangkok.

In fact the early days of *Tomorrow Never Dies* were beset with problems. Squabbles broke out between writer Bruce Feirstein and director Roger Spottiswoode, placing cast members in difficulty as they tried to cope with last-minute rewrites. Moreover, the race to get the film out and into the cinemas to capture vital Christmas audiences took the spend over the $100 million budget. Even Brosnan, it was rumoured, fell prey to the malaise, finding it hard at times to get along with Teri Hatcher, while she was said to have complained about him, as well as her part, which she felt was too small.

Brosnan was reunited with his Bond regulars from *GoldenEye*: Judi Dench as M; Desmond Llewelyn, though at the time eighty-two years old, as Q; and Samantha Bond as Miss Moneypenny. Geoffrey Palmer, whose urbane humour was well known to British television viewers of *As Time Goes By* (and in which, incidentally, he co-starred with Judy Dench), was recruited to play the bluff yet patriotic Admiral Roebuck, who would attempt to overrule M in a vital crisis. The German actor, Gotz Otto, well known for stage and screen work in his native country, was cast as Stamper, Elliot Carver's chief thug.

Brosnan was also joined by three female newcomers. This was Bond girl power with a difference. Teri Hatcher, who during the making of the film was voted the world's sexiest woman, had already gained popularity for her regular Saturday morning television appearances as Lois Lane in *Lois and Clark: The New Adventures of Superman*. She played the part of Paris Carver, a former girlfriend of Bond, who has since become married to the villain of the piece. This was Elliot Carver, played by the formidable Jonathan Pryce, who had recently starred opposite Madonna as

Juan Perón in *Evita*, as well as picking up Olivier and Tony Awards for his starring role in *Miss Saigon* on Broadway. In *Tomorrow Never Dies* Teri succumbs to the charms of her former lover and in doing so is murdered when villain Elliot suspects she has betrayed him.

It had been a long-held ambition of Hatcher to be in a Bond film. Her father used to take her to see earlier adventures when she was a little girl. Her actor-husband Jon Tenney, meanwhile, had said she must take the role, if only so he could say that he was married to a Bond girl.

Playing the part of Bond's female foe, Wai Lin, a Chinese secret agent, is Michelle Yeoh, a thirty-five-year old who looked much younger and was said to be the highest-paid actress in Asia. Not only does she match Bond for 'cool', but as early studio news leaks pointed out, '. . . she shoots to kill, kicks to maim and will take on any challenge, whether leaping from the forty-third storey of an office block or facing trained killers underwater'. The dark-haired former Miss Malaysia who also achieved an advanced level degree in ballet at London's Royal Academy of Dance, explained: 'They chose me because they wanted a woman of the Nineties.' Her ability and willingness to perform many of her own action sequences were said to have helped her secure the part of the beautiful, but deadly secret agent. Though totally independent the Kung-Fu-kicking Wai Lin temporarily joins forces with Bond to wage war against the common enemy. In their interaction we see clearly how Bond has been forced to move with the times. Yeoh turns down repeated efforts by Bond for them to work together, but when she finally assents, she does so on her own terms. All James's smooth, romantic flannel cuts no ice, and she remains totally independent and fearless – very much her own woman.

The third Bond girl is Cecilia Thomsen, a Danish former model, beautiful, blonde and 5 foot 10 inches tall. As Professor Inga Bergstrom, she had just one day of filming in the entire movie, and that day was spent entirely in bed with James, in the only scene she has. Top that as a story to tell your family and friends when you get home!

'This time around the Bond girls have become women of substance,' explained Brosnan. For the first time ever in a 007 movie, Bond has a meaningful relationship with one of the girls – something that never happened in the days of Connery or Moore. There was also a bonus Bond girl in *Tomorrow Never Dies*. Daphne Deckers is Dutch and plays Elliot Carver's public relations woman. At twenty-eight she was living with 1996 Wimbledon champion Richard Krajicek at the time. She auditioned for three parts in the picture and had to wait for two agonizing months before receiving the news that she had been successful in being cast in the speaking part of the PR specialist.

But it is the close and sensitive relationship between Bond and Paris Carver that is exactly the kind of change Brosnan had wanted to see in the new picture. Their relationship has an emotional depth and respect that would have been outside the remit of earlier Bonds, whose earthy entanglements were strictly physical, and constructed from a highly masculine perspective. Mind you, the new Bond's early approach work would have done credit to Connery or Moore, as he cynically reactivates an affair with Paris Carver as a means of obtaining information from her about her villainous husband. It is only after she has told him that she is not going to be used (as Bond has used women in previous films) that she eventually relents – a weakening that leads eventually to her own demise. But the nature of their intimate relationship really picks out this James Bond from the others. You sense that he genuinely cares for this woman.

The *ingénue* Lois Lane was initially hard to reconcile with the worldly Paris Carver of *Tomorrow Never Dies*, but Teri Hatcher turned out to be an inspired choice in her small, but vital role. The handling of her embrace with Brosnan, in which he gently disrobes her before the scene is cut, is both moving and sensual. With that wry smile Brosnan later said that he enjoyed working with Teri, and particularly in that scene – this despite the rumours that they did not always get along well together.

To Teri would go the distinction of creating the biggest surprise of all on the set. She was not required as the early scenes were being shot, but when she did arrive, she quietly announced to the astonishment of all that she was pregnant. Having secured the role, she admitted that she was nervous about mentioning her condition. But everyone appeared far less concerned than she was and, according to Teri, were very laid-back about it. Rumour had it that during her four months on the set, which was completed in a scheduled two stages with a break midway through for a swift return home to California, her impressive dress required only some minor adjustment on her return to work to accommodate, and discreetly disguise for filming, her gentle bulge.

Since the media has assumed such a central role in everyday life it is not altogether surprising that Bond's 'fight for right and justice' should focus on this area of business, with Communist China as a focal point. As early publicity proclaimed, *Tomorrow Never Dies* is a 'hi-tec, high octane account of media power as a lethal weapon, when global communications in the wrong hands can literally manufacture the news and even challenge the course of history. Particularly for a man who controls a global daily newspaper – circulation 100 million – and satellite systems able to access every television set on earth.'

Elliot Carver ('words are the new weapons') is the British global media mogul, a shadowy figure who is intelligent and ruthless; a pathological megalomaniac who operates from a technologically advanced 'stealth ship'. He devises a cunning plan aimed at bringing him exclusive media control of the entire world.

Carver is as evil as any of Bond's previous opponents, but his devilish scheme is not only potentially deadly, but also simple. By a deliberate and cynical manipulation of his powerful control of the media worldwide, by creating tomorrow's news today, by manufacturing catastrophic events, he is sure he will be able to become omnipotent . . . a world supremo.

China is a challenge, but Carver's clever use of technology seems all set to succeed, when a British naval frigate is mysteriously lost with all hands in Chinese waters. Carver attempts to frame China for the dastardly deed he has perpetrated, hoping that this will provoke a major military response from the West, leading to World War Three. The terrifying prospects of a nuclear war loom large. Carver's *Tomorrow* newspaper headlines the disaster: 'BRITISH SAILORS MURDERED. SEVENTEEN MACHINE-GUNNED BODIES FOUND.' It's a world exclusive. Carver's plan is to use this explosive situation to realize his evil ambition. Back in Bond country M sensibly argues against the British strategy of launching a military strike against China. Given just forty-eight hours to sort things out she assigns Bond to the job.

It's a tough one, but James is never one to shirk a challenge. He dashes into the attack, cool-headed and always controlled, even in the most hazardous situations. He cleverly succeeds in persuading Wai Lin (Michelle Yeoh), working for the People's External Security Force and who is herself on an assignment to investigate the activities of Elliot Carver, to join forces with him temporarily in the common cause. 'She is a kind of female Bond,' explained Brosnan. There develops an explosive confrontation between good and evil at Carver's headquarters in Vietnam. Bond and Wai Lin win the day and prevent a nuclear holocaust, while Carver becomes the victim of his own technology.

Total Film described it as an impressive and uproarious spy thriller, 'crammed with big-budget action sequences, mouth-watering women and a fair helping of witty one-liners.' But it also judged: 'As in *GoldenEye* the best thing on offer is still Brosnan, who switches effortlessly from ruthless professional to smooth ladies' man.' Another report picked out his relaxed technique, and the way he delivered one-liners 'with aplomb, assurance and conviction'.

The long Bond tradition of spectacular set-pieces is fully upheld in *Tomorrow Never Dies*. Among high-tension sequences are a memorable screeching car chase round the bends of a multi-storey car park in Hamburg (North London's Brent Cross shopping centre car park). This was one of a number of scenes that Brosnan found especially tiring, though he was not heavily involved personally. The sequence featured Bond's remote-controlled BMW 750iL and looked so realistic that a terrified bystander reportedly called the emergency service in a panic. To make the scene authentic, left-hand-drive cars were brought in and the English signs replaced with German ones. This latest Bond car had to embody a technological advance on its predecessors and gained full marks on that score with rockets hidden in the sun-roof, bullet-proof glass and bodywork, re-inflatable tyres, magnetic flash grenades and tear-gas mechanism, as well as many other 'secrets'. BMW were said to have provided seventeen cars for the film.

The latest Walther – this time mk P99, is still very much a deadly weapon, with an increased magazine capacity of sixteen rounds. A new telephone incorporates a fingerprint scanner, a 20,000-volt security system and a remote control for the car. It's a wonder even Bond dares to use it! A two-week stint in Thailand, at an estimated cost of $4 million, included the shooting of one of the film's most daring stunts, in which Bond and Wai Lin on a motorbike leap a hovering helicopter before resuming their journey across Vietnamese roof-tops. Some filming in Bangkok took place shortly after Pierce's nasty facial cut mentioned earlier. The fading scar was still visible and the camera crew had to take care that in any possible close-ups they showed the unaffected side of his face.

Tomorrow Never Dies would emerge as probably the most expansive yet controlled Bond film of them all. James had a fashion make-over and is seen wearing ultra-cool suits and a tailored over-coat from Brioni in Italy, shirts and ties by Turnbull and Asser, but his shoes are, as tradition demanded, from Church's of England.

Noted film critic Robert Sellers seemed to capture the view of the masses when, after seeing the new movie, he reported: 'Pierce Brosnan slots so naturally into the role of James Bond one assumes his mother bottle-fed him on vodka martinis and his pram came equipped with rocket launchers.' Further praise came when Britain's highly respected movie pundit Barry Norman announced that Pierce Brosnan was now beginning to rival Sean Connery in the Bond role. Another review was equally complimentary: 'It was an excellent performance from Brosnan – measured and confident.' Journalist Adrian Turner reported, 'Brosnan has filled Sean Connery's shoes with ease,' while Alan Stanbrook in the *Daily Telegraph* considered that, 'Pierce Brosnan is settling in well as 007, unlike everyone else since Sean Connery.'

The charity premiere of *Tomorrow Never Dies* was a glittering event held at the Odeon Cinema in Leicester Square, London. The cast, producers and directors appeared on stage to welcome the specially invited audience. It was a special moment for anyone and everyone associated with James Bond when, just in advance of the end credits, a simple dedication was read out to the assembled audience: 'In loving memory of Albert R. "Cubby" Broccoli'.

The picture was released nationwide in Britain on 12 December 1997. The promotion of the picture was a massive operation in itself. Merchandising, publishing, interviews and a host of promotional tie-ins of all kinds set new standards for their intensity and proliferation. In the United States small dolls of Bond, Wai Lin and Carver became best-sellers. A major London store had a whole series of window displays about the new film; a documentary on British television gave a rare insight into how the picture had been made. It was an operation, in its own way, almost as extensive and painstaking as the making of the film itself.

The film-makers had done a magnificent job in having the picture ready for its projected Christmas release in Britain. There was titanic competition, literally, from James Cameron's epic movie of that name – which in the United States in fact opened on the same day as *Tomorrow Never Dies*.

Titanic registered the best box office of all time, but an eventual $340 million for *Tomorrow Never Dies* made everybody happy, being only some $10 million below the *GoldenEye* mark. That, against the head-to-head opposition of *Titanic*, was considered to be a near-miracle. In the United States *Tomorrow Never Dies* became the top-grossing Bond movie with a box office take of $124 million, which was $19 million more than the figure for *GoldenEye*.

The James Bond musical themes have been an integral part of the movie presentations over the years, from Matt Monroe's vocal version of 'From Russia with Love', to 'Goldfinger' (which started the tradition of Bond Theme songs becoming popular hits). In *Tomorrow Never Dies* it is the American singer Sheryl Crow who sings the title song. Shirley Bassey's 'Diamonds Are Forever' became perhaps the most enduring, but for Brosnan fans there was by now really only one choice. With music by Marvin Hamlisch, lyrics by Carole Bayer Sayer and the singing of stylish songstress Carly Simon, it must be the Oscar-nominated theme from the 1977 Bond movie, *The Spy Who Loved Me*. The title? Of course, as any fan of Pierce Brosnan would tell you instantly, 'Nobody Does It Better'.

12

Not Just a Star

THAT THERE COULD BE EVEN a remote connection between the small, coastal town of Hastings in East Sussex, and James Bond, aka Pierce Brosnan, seems implausible. The two are worlds apart. Hastings, though a modern enough town for the new millennium, is still known primarily for the famous battle of 1066 that took place just six miles away in which the Saxon King Harold met his death from an arrow in his eye. Battle Abbey commemorates the site.

Agent 007 came from another age, another world. Brosnan had doubtless never even considered visiting Hastings. But a strong connection between the two would certainly became established in 1998. Even more remarkable, perhaps, is that it was a man who was born 110 years earlier and died in 1938 that would provide the inspiration.

Archie Belaney was born in Hastings to a teenage mother in the early hours of 18 September 1888 and was cared for in his infancy by two kind-hearted maiden aunts, Ada and Carrie. This was the Victorian age with its rigid regimes, when children were strongly disciplined and led a life in which any wayward instincts were crushed by adults. Archie found solace in books. He read everything he could about nature, animals and wildlife in general and dreamed about the day he might escape to a new life in Canada, where he could be near to the natural world that meant so much to him.

Archie was a quiet, solitary boy who derived much pleasure from reading the adventure stories that then appeared regularly in children's magazines. He was captivated by stories of the Wild West and the battles between American Indians and white settlers. By the time he was eleven he was deeply fascinated by woods and wild animals, and loved to go camping and trekking. Often he would pretend to be a Native American, tracking animals. Even at this tender age he appeared to have a special rapport with animals. He once found a snake and took it home, where it became a devoted pet.

Instinctively, the young Archie Belaney was a loner and loved to explore the woods on his own. Though largely introspective in day-to-day life, he was said to have had a definite talent for acting and a rare gift for parody. When playing a part he was not self-conscious in the slightest. His feeling for the written word extended beyond reading about natural history, and during the 1930s, in his forties, he went on to write five books, all of which were published in Britain, the United States and Canada, and all highly respected.

Archie Belaney's remarkable story began to unfold significantly one afternoon in March 1906 when, just seventeen, and with his interest having now developed into an obsession, he set sail from Liverpool docks on the Dominion Line steamship *Canada*, bound for Halifax, where he disembarked en route for Toronto. It was the start of what would later become widely accepted as one of the most extraordinary adventure stories of the twentieth century.

More than ninety years on, the 44-year-old Pierce Brosnan had just completed his final scenes for the James Bond blockbuster, *Tomorrow Never Dies*. His lucrative contract had already secured his immediate future as 007, so when choosing his next film project he was able to take his pick from any number of potential blockbusters. Instead he chose to work on a modest movie about a real-life character called Grey Owl, who had found fame in Britain and around the world in the 1930s.

Grey Owl would later come to be considered as the first ever eco-warrior, mainly because of his courageous and sustained fight to save the beavers in Northern Ontario, Canada, from possible extinction. He also took his pioneering message of conservation around the world. Visiting Britain twice, the second time in 1937, he gave a series of talks at a number of venues, explaining how he had grown up among the Ojibway Indians, the son of an Apache mother and a Scottish father who had fought with Buffalo Bill. He described his home as a simple shack by a lake, in the deeply remote wilderness of Saskatchewan. Here he lived at one with the wildlife, 'calling the birds from the trees and conjuring beavers to his table'.

Earlier he had been a trapper, riverman and fire-ranger and became noted both for his daring and for the remarkable attraction women had for him. He was said to have had five wives, not always one at a time, and four children. It was only after meeting and marrying a twenty-year-old American Indian girl called Anahareo that he was persuaded by her to give up trapping. The two of them thereafter began working for the protection of animals and land conservation.

Brosnan found the whole story of Grey Owl totally absorbing. 'It has everything,' he declared, 'drama, human conflict, adventure and historical fact.' He learned about the enormous impact Grey Owl had created with his talks when, wearing full Indian head-dress, he had packed theatres and halls on that amazingly successful tour of Britain in 1937. All sixty appearances had been sold out.

The fame of Grey Owl and his extraordinary lifestyle reached its peak in December of that year, when he was invited to

Buckingham Palace. There, in the Throne Room, he met not only King George VI and Queen Elizabeth (the present Queen Mother), but also their two young daughters, Elizabeth (now Queen) and Princess Margaret.

A BBC2 *Timewatch* programme in 1999 revealed something of Grey Owl's arrogance. Even at the palace he had insisted on a uniquely dramatic entrance. Not for Grey Owl the then traditional custom of waiting in an ante-chamber until, with appropriate dignity and ceremony, the arrival of Their Majesties was announced. Grey Owl insisted on reversing the procedure so that he could be announced to the already assembled Royal hosts. As the *Radio Times* explained many years later: 'When all was ready the doors were flung open by a footman and in strode a tall, dark-skinned man of grave and spiritual cast, dressed in a buckskin jacket and moccasins and wearing a single feather in his long, plaited hair.' He is said to have approached King George VI and raised his hand: 'How Kola. My name is Wa-Sha-Quon-Asin . . . Grey Owl!' He went on to detail just how he had become Grey Owl and much later declared that Princess Elizabeth 'was the most attentive young lady who ever came to one of my lectures'.

It was also in 1937 during the same tour, on a cold, uninviting night in Leicester, that the brothers Attenborough, David and Richard, sat in awe as they listened attentively to Grey Owl telling his remarkable and inspiring story. The authorized version of the life and times of Grey Owl had almost run its course. But despite the subsequent revelations, David Attenborough commented: 'I was enormously impressed. Along with other things, he inspired me to an interest in nature.' Brother Richard also sustained a long-term interest in Grey Owl and went on to direct the film about him.

Within two years, Grey Owl suddenly fell seriously ill and died, in 1938. He was just fifty years old and only then, within a dramatically short time of his death, did the true story emerge.

Dante's Peak (1997) was something of a landmark movie for Brosnan. His sensitive portrayal in the lead role as the cool, intellectual volcano expert Dr Harry Dalton added substantially to his credentials as a serious actor. It was a big-budget movie from a major Hollywood studio and grossed almost $500 million worldwide. Linda Hamilton played a single mother, Jeremy Foley and Jamie Rence Smith her children

As bar owner Joe Brady in *The Nephew* (1998) with his free-spirited screen daughter Aislin McGuckin. Mainstream movies aside, Brosnan was determined to make the kind of small films he felt ought to be made... 'movies with heart'. Made by his own production company, *The Nephew* marked his début as a film producer

Racing back as Bond in *Tomorrow Never Dies* (1997). New style Bond girl Wai Lin (actress Michelle Yeoh) plays her part in James's all-action plan to save the world. Film critic Robert Sellers commented: 'Pierce Brosnan slots so naturally into the role of James Bond one assumes his mother bottle-fed him on vodka martinis and his pram came equipped with rocket launchers'

(Brosnan and Yeoh still photograph from the motion picture *Tomorrow Never Dies*

In the successful remake of *The Thomas Crown Affair* (1999), Brosnan stars as a self-styled billionaire who has run out of challenges and peps up his life by lifting a priceless Monet from a world-famous museum. He co-produced the movie with business partner Beau St Clair, through their own production company, Irish Dream Time

With Denise Richards in the 1999 Bond blockbuster, *The World Is Not Enough*. The picture underlined his overwhelming international acceptance as agent 007. He was also influential in bringing the most successful film franchise up to date, in keeping with the approach of the year 2000 (Brosnan and Richards still photograph from the motion picture *The World is Not Enough* © 1999 Danjaq, LLC and United Artists Corporation. All rights reserved)

Pierce with Keely Shaye-Smith, whom he married in August 2001. Their steady and dedicated relationship grew out of a casual meeting some three years after the death of his wife Cassie. Their sons Dylan and Paris were born in January 1997 and February 2001 respectively

Bike shop owner Owen Miles had the surprise of his life when Pierce Brosnan walked in. 007 was on a mission in Street, Somerset, to obtain a suitable bike for his son, Sean, who was a pupil at a nearby school

There was no doubt that Grey Owl had done most of what he claimed he had done. He had an exceptionally intense affinity with wildlife. He was a pioneer conservationist and a strong opponent of deforestation, boldly taking his message around the world at a time when such views would have branded him as a crank in some quarters. Certainly, he was married to Anahareo, and it was largely through her influence that he saved the Canadian beaver, which until then had been hunted close to extinction. The story goes that the caring Anahareo came across two beaver kittens which were caught in brutal traps. She pleaded with Grey Owl to save them with such intensity and anguish that he felt obliged to comply; in so doing, he changed the course of his life forever.

But although he was known as Grey Owl, he was certainly not an American Indian; nor had he ever been one. He was not the son of an Apache mother and his so-called Scottish father had never seen Buffalo Bill, let alone fought with him. His tanned skin was said to have come from a sun-lamp, and his magnificent native dress had been bought in London's Regent Street. Grey Owl – real name Archie Belaney – had in fact been cared for as a child by two maiden aunts in the East Sussex town of Hastings.

With such a story little wonder Brosnan was captivated by the prospect of portraying Grey Owl. He quickly decided it was a role he was determined to secure, telling his agent in Los Angeles that he was prepared to audition, attend meetings and have a screen test – all of which might have seemed demeaning for an actor of twenty years' experience and a James Bond on the crest of a wave. 'I identified so much with the whole thing,' he explained. But Brosnan had no cause for concern; the film company had already decided they wanted him. 'The part is yours,' said his agent. 'It's a firm offer.'

Belaney's clever deception was extraordinary because of its complete success over so many years and because of his deep and honest feelings for nature and conservation. As Grey Owl, his heart was in the right place, and those who felt charitably towards him suggested that there had been no malicious intent in his audacious hoax. He had done no real harm, indeed had done an enormous amount of good in terms of the preservation of wildlife. The subterfuge had been no more than a means to an end, a clever strategy that had enabled him to get his message across with conviction. For as one observer remarked, 'Who would have believed him if he had turned up to give his talks in a tailored suit with a buttoned-up shirt and a tie, and announcing that as a child he had lived in Hastings?'

Astonishingly, neither did his wife have any idea of his original identity until near the end of his life. Even more remarkable was that a disgruntled former wife of Grey Owl had told a Canadian newspaper reporter about his real identity as long ago as 1935, three years before his death, but on the instructions of his editor the story was not permitted to be released during Belaney's lifetime. Within days of his death the startling news was out.

The story was powerful and dramatic, yet tender and endearing. 'It is like our own love story,' Brosnan told his, by now, long-time partner Keely Shaye-Smith, both of whom at the time were basking in the joy of their seventeen-month-old son, Dylan Thomas. For, in several ways Pierce and Keely would find resonances with Grey Owl's story in their beliefs and the way they conducted their lives. Brosnan said: 'Keely has worked hard for the preservation of dolphins and whales and we both believe that conservation and the environment are vital.' Pierce seemed truly inspired by Grey Owl's life and was enchanted by the love story at its heart. He pointed out the uncanny similarities – how, like him, Grey Owl had met a woman who was to change his life, and how, like him, Grey Owl had come to regard conservation and the environment as vital issues for the future.

He would almost have taken the part without payment. The fact that Sir Richard Attenborough would be directing the movie was an enormous boost. The man who had become legendary in movie-making for such epics as *A Bridge Too Far* in 1977, *Gandhi* (1982) and *Cry Freedom* (1987) was, at seventy-five years old, still an inspiration to Pierce Brosnan, with whom he had never worked before. 'The man is a legend and I had long wanted to work with him,' revealed Brosnan.

The *Timewatch* programme explained how, in 1937, Grey Owl had made a controversial recording for BBC's *Children's Hour* in which he fiercely opposed the hunting of foxes, otters and hares. He had refused the Corporation's request to omit a passage that they considered could be offensive to some listeners, so the broadcast did not go ahead. Yet interestingly, when the banned talk was put out as a pamphlet by Grey Owl's own publishers, it sold an astonishing 50,000 copies; and some sixty years later the offending talk was included in the 1999 *Timewatch* programme.

Archie Belaney's astounding deception gave the Grey Owl story its added dimension. David Attenborough explained that the fact that Belaney said he was a Native American Indian gave a certain glamour to his story, but the important issue for him was that here was an individual who said that it was cruel to trap beavers, who understood them and lived in the wilderness. 'That was enough for me,' he declared.

It was for similar reasons that the debonair James Bond, repeated saviour of the world, would find himself in 1998 quietly tucked away in a log cabin in the middle of a dense Canadian forest, wearing a buckskin tunic, his skin darkened by a special pigment and with hair extensions firmly glued into place. Anne Galipeau, a member of the Algonquin tribe, was cast as Brosnan's screen wife, Anahareo. Brosnan later travelled to Hastings for two weeks of filming in the authentic birthplace of Archie Belaney.

In going for the role of Grey Owl, Pierce Brosnan had stuck to his declared intention of not only doing those movies which had a high profile, but also more minor movies that appealed personally to him, widened his horizons or presented some particular challenge to him as an actor. Lavish blockbusters like James Bond were not his only way of life. But while *Grey Owl* would be sluggish in finding its way into cinemas countrywide, the process of making movies continued for Brosnan at a rapid pace. Not only would two Brosnan films now be released within the short space of seven or eight months during the latter part of 1999, but both of them were of sufficient mass appeal to raise the actor's media profile significantly.

Pierce was now sizing up projects not only as an actor, but also as a director and producer, both of which he now had some experience. In the past he had never shown any inclination to return to old ideas. Sequels held little interest for him. But that was to change significantly one morning when he was having coffee with Beau St Clair, his co-producing partner in Irish Dream Time – their joint film production company. 'We were just chatting casually about remakes when the old 1968 Steve McQueen–Faye Dunaway movie, *The Thomas Crown Affair*, came up,' he revealed.

Having decided to launch Irish Dream Time with the modest *The Nephew*, St Clair and Brosnan were already on the look-out for a suitable second project. They soon realized that a remake of *The Thomas Crown Affair* was a distinct possibility. 'I immediately thought that Pierce would be ideal as Thomas Crown,' said St Clair. 'It could be a natural for him.' Brosnan recalled: 'Both she and I had seen the original movie and loved it.' The project became gradually more tangible the more they thought about it. St Clair said: 'We both thought it would be a wonderful challenge to incorporate the themes and conflicts of the old movie into something contemporary and original.'

To turn the idea into reality required the backing of a major studio. Brosnan was now a very bankable star, MGM liked the idea and gave Irish Dream Time the green light to go ahead on the £40 million project. Brosnan said at the time: 'Within two years we were in production. The essential work in between began with the writing of a completely new script.'

This time round Thomas Crown is a self-made billionaire who organizes the theft of a $100 million Monet canvas for excitement, because it is both a challenge and something money cannot buy. Alan R. Trustman had written the original 1968 script out of his work as a banker, but for the updated version, two new writers, Leslie Dixon and Kurt Wimmer, were engaged. They had not worked together before and came together for this one assignment only. Once satisfied with their script, Brosnan sent it off to director John McTiernan. He and Brosnan had worked together on the 1986 thriller, *Nomads*. So impressed was McTiernan with the updated version's possibilities that he committed himself to the new film overnight. Brosnan and Beau St Clair officially became joint producers of the new project.

It was the subtle but significant way in which the remake differed from the original that captured McTiernan's interest. 'The original *The Thomas Crown Affair* was primarily a caper film,' he explained, 'but this is a romance.' So said the director who had successfully steered such major productions as *Die Hard* and *Die Hard: With a Vengeance*, as well as *The Hunt For Red October*. 'It's about two hard cases, two people who are very good being successful singles and very bad at sustained relationships.' McTiernan added: 'I liked the love story, the "Taming of the Shrew" aspect of it. You have two people who are, in their own way, brutally successful. But that same cold independence that works for them professionally, makes them failures at having a relationship. These two could only get together in the middle of very dangerous circumstances.'

As the pieces started falling into place, Brosnan began to relish the idea of portraying a forceful financier whose primary weapon is his intellect. 'I had long thought that Thomas Crown was one of the truly clever and complex characters in the literature of cinema,' he commented. 'He is a powerful man for whom winning is not enough; he craves the stimulation of a good gambit – the more dangerous, the better. Moreover, this is a man with no apparent vulnerabilities, guarded even in the presumed sanctuary of his psychiatrist's office.'

The fabulously wealthy Thomas Crown can buy anything he wants and is irresistible to women, but he is bored with his life and decides to do something about it. When an alarm sounds at a world-class museum and someone walks out with a priceless Monet, Crown is the last person the New York police suspects. But one person does suspect him: Catherine Banning, the brilliant female insurance investigator hired to retrieve the painting no matter what it takes. Catherine loves the chase as much as he does and she is on to his game. Crown has found his ultimate challenge. As the film's strapline teased: 'Two can play, but only one can win.'

The casting of the role of Banning (opposite Brosnan) was crucial. The female role was almost as important to the success of the movie as Thomas Crown himself. She needed to be attractive, tough and experienced. Not too young, flippant or pretty-pretty. Said Brosnan: 'What Crown sees in Catherine is a way out of his life. When he falls in love with her he sees his mirror image.' An actress who had portrayed smart, tough women throughout her remarkable career is Rene Russo. Though aged forty-five – Dunaway was twenty-seven when she took the corresponding role in the 1968 version – Russo was offered the role and accepted immediately. Having starred with Mel Gibson in sequels 3 and 4 of *Lethal Weapon* and with Gibson again successfully in Ron Howard's *Ransom*, she quickly got to the bottom of her new Banning character. 'Catherine has the instincts of a bounty hunter and the determination of a dedicated cop,' she suggested. 'She is accustomed to being able to outwit, outmanoeuvre and outlast any white-collar criminal she encounters. But in *Crown* she makes the big mistake of thinking she can get close enough for the capture without falling for him.'

Russo has often had to play down the glamour in many of her earlier movie roles, so the former fashion model welcomed the opportunity to look smart, sophisticated and well made-up in *Thomas Crown*. 'It's also the first film where I can put a little sexual energy into the role,' she declared. The critical scene comes midway through the movie. Banning creates a sensation at a 'black and white' charity ball in an almost transparent eye-catching gown. Seeing Crown dancing with a younger woman she moves in for the kill. She was to prove the excellence of her casting, the special chemistry between her and Brosnan charging the film with a powerfully sensual undertone. Catherine Banning was described as a sexual predator, and shooting the ballroom scene in which the chic insurance investigator's pursuit of Crown turns to seduction was said to be difficult for her, since Russo is a dedicated Christian. She told a Los Angeles reporter: 'Taking my clothes off was not something I did lightly. I prayed about it and I thought about it. It was an emotional roller-coaster for me.'

For Brosnan, *The Thomas Crown Affair* was a very different type of challenge from his portrayal as the Native American environmental activist pioneer in *Grey Owl* – or indeed from the lavish, thundering action of Bond. It was also his second project as a producer, here sharing the responsibilities as co-producer with Beau St Clair. The Thomas Crown role was seen to be ideal for Brosnan and he underplayed the softly spoken, ice-cool gentleman crook, to perfection. Said one report: 'Brosnan is perfectly cast as Thomas Crown, the self-made billionaire out for some action and excitement in his life.' Another judged: 'Brosnan steps into Steve McQueen's shoes with unexpected success'; while a third review suggested that he fitted into the role with 'consummate ease'.

But as anyone who saw the original version will know, the story's ultimate success depends heavily on the sexual chemistry of the two protagonists. Bob McCabe in *Empire* pinpointed this issue well. 'Brosnan is all graceful elegance and smouldering charm, a

167

confident, attractive man who even manages to push the presence of Bond out of the frame, while Russo is a veritable cat on heat, all smouldering sensuality, masking potential vulnerability.' Comparisons with the earlier classic were inevitable, and in the head-to-head contest between the famous sexy chess scene in the earlier movie and the equivalent dance sequence in the remake, Brosnan and Russo seemed to have the edge for most reviewers.

The leads in both versions of the film were all classy performers; if anything, it was in the sexual chemistry that the remake had the edge. But as a kind of affectionate tribute to the original, the new *Crown* film had Faye Dunaway playing a cameo role as a psychiatrist; the tune chosen for the big dance sequence, meanwhile, and indeed the closing credits, was the Michel Legrand, Marilyn Bergman and Alan Bergman classic song from the original movie, 'The Windmills of Your Mind', in the later version sung by Sting, over the closing credits.

The basic story, updated, held its ground remarkably well after more than thirty years. Director John McTiernan explained: 'We changed the character from the original to a man who had made money himself. He came from nowhere, got himself to Oxford on a boxing scholarship and took that pugnacity to just push further ahead. Twenty years later, he is in his mid-forties, he's got his fortune and he's kicked the hell out of just about everybody he's come up against.' It is then that the tight-lipped, merciless financier creates his own challenge.

The film was shot largely around Manhattan and Westchester County, New York, with location work in the Caribbean. It was during location filming on the island of Martinique that five men tried to mug Rene and a girlfriend. 'One grabbed me and tried to get my purse, but I yelled so loud that they all ran off; but my girlfriend's purse was snatched.'

Not surprisingly, the sumptuous trappings of Crown's billionaire lifestyle figure prominently. His superb Fifth Avenue mansion on New York's Upper East Side had to reflect the right balance of nouveau aristocratic elegance and idosyncratic art connoisseurship that, according to production designer Bruno Rubeo, formed the essence of someone who is essentially a very private man. 'It's not just a rich man's home,' explained Rubeo. 'Crown is a very eccentric guy with particular tastes and a particular lifestyle. You have to come up with the right mood to create that idea.'

The whole thing in fact was created by transforming a warehouse in Yonkers situated on the Hudson River in New York State. The entrance to Crown Towers, corporate headquarters of the Crown empire, was shot in an unoccupied office building near the New York Stock Exchange, while the corporate headquarters of Lucent Technologies stood in for Crown's suite of offices in Crown Towers. The outside of the National Arts Club, where Crown arranges his first date with Catherine, was the India Club in Hanover Square.

By far the greatest challenge was how to film the museum interior scenes. McTiernan's exasperation told its own story. 'You probably can't get permission to film an art theft in any major museum in the world,' he explained. 'They have huge security systems and they're very secretive about how those operate. They also can't insure valuable art works against potential damage from film crews working around them; nor could we, because one wrecked painting could see off the budget for the entire film.' In the end an entire set-up was created in a former Subaru dealership next to the warehouse soundstages. The original 150 master prints were reproduced by a team of twenty Parisian artists working over a four-month period and to a budget of $200,000. The only exception to a set built from scratch was the final scene, in which Crown enters the museum ostensibly to return the stolen Monet. For this scene the film-makers converted the entrance of the New York Public Library into the entrance for their museum.

Location work on the French-speaking Caribbean resort island of Martinique seemed like a welcome change of scenery and climate for Brosnan, Russo and other members of the cast and crew. The more relaxed atmosphere was somewhat undermined, however, by inaccessible locations and unpredictable weather. And the attempted mugging of Russo and her friend left a nasty taste. Surprisingly perhaps, Crown's athletic pursuits were not filmed there. The scenes of golf, gliding and catamaran racing were filmed in Westchester County and Connecticut.

Doing a remake of any film is a risky business. Film-makers need to have a very good reason indeed for re-creating a movie that has flopped. To redo a movie that has already been successful, and which starred such Hollywood legends as Steve McQueen and Faye Dunaway, was indeed a courageous and, some might say, foolhardy move. But as one critic pointed out: 'Ignoring the original, *The Thomas Crown Affair* could easily have been written with Brosnan in mind.' Brosnan himself was by no means intimidated by the movie's history. 'I know expectations are high,' he said just before the latest picture was released. 'I'm a big Steve McQueen fan, he was a great actor. But I don't see myself as a replica and in any event it is thirty years since the last version. There's a whole generation out there that doesn't know the film.'

In this case the gamble of reworking a well-loved film certainly paid off handsomely. The critics were largely enthusiastic, and the public were attracted to see it, so that it stayed well up in the charts for many weeks. *The Thomas Crown Affair* was released in August 1999 and had its international premiere at that year's Edinburgh International Film Festival.

13
The Man Behind the Star

THERE IS A COMPLEXITY ABOUT Pierce Brosnan that singles him out from the galaxy of mainstream Hollywood stars. He is versatile, yet strongly focused; ambitious yet often diffident. Although a dedicated Catholic, he none the less stubbornly resisted his conscience by 'living in sin' with new girlfriend Keely Shaye-Smith. Don't ever try to impress by calling him a big Hollywood star. He would much rather you told him, with candour, what you thought of his performance. He loves being James Bond and may well continue in the role until someone tells him it is time to stop; but that is just as likely to be his inner self as Eon Productions.

You also get the feeling, were it not essential for the job, that he would much prefer to put on his coat once filming a movie was over and depart for home and family, rather than go through all the high jinks of personal appearances and media interviews which are now an essential part of life as a Hollywood superstar. In this sense he has carried over some of the trappings of the traditional Hollywood star of the 1930s. Movie idols in those days could retreat from the public gaze between pictures and happily cocoon themselves in their Beverly Hills mansions until their next picture brought them out into the open again. By today's standards he is very much a private person.

For all his comparatively recent fame Pierce Brosnan remains largely the same man he was before. He speaks softly and leads a quiet personal life. The stepchildren he inherited from his marriage to Cassandra are now grown up, but they are still very much part of his, and Keely's, life. Charlotte, twenty-five years old when Pierce was making *Tomorrow Never Dies*, was working in London at the time, so they had the opportunity to meet from time to time. Christopher, a year younger, and having graduated from being a production runner on *GoldenEye*, was then working as one of fourteen additional assistant directors on the latest Bond movie. Stepfather and stepson had their own responsibilities, but working together on the same project brought a closeness that they both valued. Sean, then thirteen years old, was based with his father in London for the duration of the film, and Pierce, after a heavy day of shooting at Leavesden Studios, or even returning from location, would take Sean and his tutor out to a nearby restaurant to eat – or would simply enjoy spending a relaxed evening at home with his young son and friends.

Charlotte and Christopher had accompanied Pierce to the glittering London premiere of *GoldenEye* in 1995, along with his mother May and Keely. 'It's good to have everyone around me,' Pierce told a reporter with obvious satisfaction. He makes no secret of how much he loves family life. It is because he is such a dedicated family man that he was delighted at the prospect of taking the lead in *Dante's Peak*. It had spectacular scenes and lots of vivid action, but Pierce saw it as being essentially a family movie. 'I was meant to be a family man,' he announced simply in 1997. 'I enjoy being a family man . . . I just love my family.'

This sense of blood kinship, which might well have originated in the absence of his own mother and father in those early years, made the shock loss of Cassandra so early in their lives all the more traumatic. He once explained just how tough it was being a single parent, because, as he put it, 'you are suddenly mum and you are still dad.' But he handled those vital additional responsibilities, at a time of enormous grief, with an inner strength, as indeed he appears to approach his career and life itself.

It never seemed to matter to him too much that even as recently as six years ago, despite having made twelve movies in the space of fourteen years, most movie-goers would have found it hard to put a name to his face. *Remington Steele* lifted his profile somewhat. And with the approach of the new millennium, branded and fully blooded as Bond with three sensationally successful 007 movies to his credit (*The World Is Not Enough* went on release in November 1999), along with other high-profile parts, Brosnan is a potent force in film-making. But as Shirley Eaton, one of the original Bond girls from *Goldfinger*, will tell you, he remains 'one of the nicest people you could meet, in or out of showbiz'.

He is also probably one of the most up-front superstars in the business as well as being one of the most reasoned and shrewd. This apparent contradiction again may well have its origins in his difficult childhood, the feeling of being abandoned. For a time he was left to find his own way, to set his own standards. He is said to be amiable, but at times distant. He has no reputation for being an enthusiastic party-goer or an extrovert. As often suggested by his screen persona, he would sooner underplay his success than blow his own trumpet. He is said to have a twinkle in his eye and a sharp wit.

For a star who is happy with his image, he is not dictated by it. By most accepted standards he is outrageously handsome, yet he never appears to trade on his looks. 'I just scrub up well,' he says disarmingly. He was determined to become an actor who could really act and secure roles on his ability. Indeed the breadth and variety of roles he has taken prove that Brosnan's ambitions have not been entirely in vain – and that his triumphs have not been down to his handsome features alone.

He loves the United States and felt comfortable and happy there right from the start, but he steadfastly stands aside from the super-ficiality and gossipy tittle-tattle of Hollywood. He has enthusiastically adopted Britain, too, and recognizes its special values and traditions: 'I love London and have a great fondness for England.' And he maintains a deep love for his native Ireland – '. . . it's where my spirit and soul came from.'

Despite the enormous success and the multi-million dollar excitement of James Bond, probably the highest-profile role in pictures today, he can still find deep and genuine satisfaction from the modest offerings created by his own production company, Irish Dream Time. *The Nephew* was a typical example. Put together on a tiny budget compared to the Bond movies, the picture presented Pierce with the challenge of being producer at the same time as acting in it. He explained at the time: '*The Nephew* has a decency and honesty about it, which is what I like in a film.' When he has every right to be impossibly over-confident, he seems to remain improbably self-deprecating.

Brosnan continues to hang his head in amused embarrassment when reminded of the time he guest-starred on *The Muppet Show* on television. On-screen he took the traditional punishment and humiliation like a true pro, and in the process seemed supremely relaxed, implying that he might even have enjoyed being made fun of.

His reputed amiability becomes badly stretched when challenged about the incompatibility of his religious beliefs and his intimate life with Keely outside marriage. It is clear he is not to be bullied on this or any other subject on which he might have firm views. In 1997 he told a reporter sternly, 'I'll find the altar in my own good time. Keely and I aren't ready yet.' He explained that simply because you are married doesn't guarantee a wonderful relationship; the piece of paper isn't important. Though his film persona is public property, he believes that he is entitled to a certain privacy. You got the feeling then that when he and Keely did decide to marry the invitations would not be extended to *Hello!* magazine. However, his fans were in for a surprise . . .

Friends and colleagues find the constant rehearsal of the so-called anomalies of his life vaguely amusing. The Irish background is one. Sure, as a twelve-year-old attending a Putney comprehensive for the first time, he tried to conceal his Irish origins because he did not want to be seen to be different. 'There was a good deal of prejudice even then,' he remembers. He admits that for many years after, if not exactly denying his Irish roots, he certainly did nothing to bring them to the surface. 'A bit sad,' he now reflects on those years. But he has grown to be comfortable and happy about his Irish background, though the faint trace of accent in the voice only just gives it away.

The astrologists would have a field day with Pierce Brosnan. His birth on 16 May 1953 places him firmly under the sign of Taurus, thus endowing him with, as positive traits, a warm and determined personality, while on the negative side he is classed as being stubborn and possessive. Not too far off the mark, on reflection.

Pierce's marriage to Cassandra Harris has continued to be a source of intermittent interest to the media, even now that eight years have passed since her death – and doubtless the curiosity has been fuelled by his more recent relationship with Keely Shaye-Smith. Of more enduring importance to him personally, however, was the love and devotion they had for each other and the influence that Cassie had on him and, particularly, his career. It was she who had the vision to transcend what seemed to be impossible odds, and the courage to act on her beliefs. The outcome put Brosnan securely on the road to movie stardom. It was she who took out a second mortgage on the central heating and who managed to persuade the bank to hand over £2,000. With sandwiches packed for the journey, she it was who supplied the confidence and resolve that Brosnan so palpably lacked at that stage as, striding into the unknown, they boarded that budget-priced Freddie Laker flight to California. Cassie's positive feelings were to be fully vindicated within just two weeks, when Pierce secured that coveted role in *Remington Steele*. Thereafter the couple started building a deeply loving and, with the proceeds from those regular television appearances from 1982 to 1987, prosperous life together. But he shudders to think what might have happened without that early breakthrough. He has never failed to express openly his love for Cassie and in spirit she remains an important part of his life to this day.

Not having had much of a stable family early in his own life merely emphasized Cassie's importance. Those close to him would vouch for his total sincerity when he once said: 'I cherish Cassie, Charlotte and Christopher.' That was obviously before Sean was born and of course before Dylan Thomas arrived. For all the love and affection he obviously feels for Keely, and the vital importance he places on their lives together, he has never allowed his time with Cassie to be devalued or forgotten and will always talk openly about her.

When not filming and when commitments allow, he loves to paint and reportedly has a strong talent. He relishes the quiet contemplation and solitary concentration that it demands as much as he enjoys the excitement, tension and the testing demands of high-profile film-making. Over the years he has honed his natural talent and abiding interest in art that led him as a school-leaver to consider it seriously as a career, as he worked in his first job in a studio in south London. It was painting that helped save his sanity in those awful days when Cassie was so ill. During the periods when the pain eased for a while and she felt a little better, he would retire to his studio in an adjoining room and, with canvas, pencil and brush, attempt to gain a sense of balance. It was a kind of therapy to which he returned once Cassie had died and he was left to rebuild his life.

First impressions on meeting Brosnan are invariably good. A

classic encounter was when former Bond girl Shirley Eaton met him for the first time at the Odeon in London's Leicester Square at a special gathering to celebrate the life and work of Cubby Broccoli. Shirley explained: 'It was obviously a very sad occasion, sombre, quiet and respectful, since Cubby was no longer with us; but it was also a happy one because Cubby had made such an enormous contribution to the business of film-making and because his life had meant so much to all of us who were there. We all said our piece, remembering Cubby in our own special and individual way.'

For Pierce and Shirley there was a shared personal resonance at the time. 'We had both recently lost loved ones,' explained Shirley. 'I had met my late husband Colin when I was nineteen and he died thirty-eight years later. Pierce was still grieving from the loss of Cassie. We just hugged each other. He is a wonderful man and a very special person.' They met again at a special showing of *Tomorrow Never Dies*. 'Everyone says what a nice man Pierce is and it is true,' explained Shirley. 'There is much more to him than those handsome features. He has charm, is genuinely interested in people and has humility, a quality not over-common in today's world of high profile, global movie-making . . . I think he has done a magnificent job as 007. He is just so right as today's James Bond and now I couldn't really see anyone else in the part. In my opinion he has justifiably made the part his own. I also happen to think that because he looks so good he could be in danger of becoming under-valued as an actor, and that would be a great pity as well as an enormous injustice.'

Shirley became internationally famous for creating probably one of the most memorable images in the history of the movies, when, as the free-spirited, beautiful blonde Jill Masterson, she appeared in *Goldfinger* in 1964 wearing nothing but a tiny G-string and a thin coating of gold 'paint', which was actually gold make-up. This led to her becoming one of the most photographed actresses of the sixties, especially when the film original was re-created for a cover shot for *Life* magazine. Talking from her home in North London she is obviously still astonished at the longevity of that now famous scene. 'You know, I made twenty-nine films in just fourteen years, yet in *Goldfinger* I was in two short scenes and on screen for less than five minutes and I'm remembered all over the world,' she explained. 'It is unbelievable . . . all of thirty-five years later and people still talk and write about it. I'm very flattered.'

Not surprisingly Sean Connery, who was Bond in the movie that brought her fame, holds a special place in Shirley's memories; so does Roger Moore. She and Colin, when they lived in the South of France in a 300-year-old farmhouse with views of the coastline as far as St-Tropez, would often have Roger and his then wife (Luisa) come to visit them.

For years there was almost universal acceptance that nobody could equal Sean Connery as Bond. He was the definitive, the archetypal Bond, the best, there had ever been and ever would be. Brosnan agreed: 'Connery was my Bond, although Roger brought a certain style and humour to the role.' But now? Could it be said that Brosnan is beginning to change all that, that Sean's lofty position is perhaps not quite as impregnable as it once was?

Certainly Pierce Brosnan is now widely accepted as the automatic choice for the part. He has grown into the role impressively, and after only three outings with at least one more to come, he has already done what many critics felt to be impossible and made James Bond synonymous with Pierce Brosnan as Sean Connery did some thirty-five years before.

Such comparisons are meaningless to Brosnan, and he doesn't feel competitive with any of his forebears. In any event he does not see James Bond as dominating his life or career. The world is full of opportunities, even for a 47-year-old (in May 2000) film actor. He took the lead in *Grey Owl* because he is fascinated by conservation and considers these things to be important enough to the human race to give some of his time to these areas of life. He has, as mentioned, championed Keely's work in the preservation of dolphins and whales, and he does all he can to help in the fight against cancer.

Pierce Brosnan is a self-confessed James Bond 'junkie' and loves the role, but he also wants to continue to do other things, some with his own production company. He is by no means a 'treadmill' movie actor, rushing to take every part that is offered to him. But one thing is certain: James Bond will assure Pierce Brosnan a unique place in motion picture history. For once that fourth James Bond movie has been released he will have the distinction of being the actor who took 007 from the twentieth century into the twenty-first.

Even Ian Fleming would have been impressed.

14
The Ubiquitous Bond

A SINGULAR WONDER OF THE FILM WORLD is the way in which a forthcoming James Bond movie can whip up such enormous speculation and interest. It defies all logic. More than thirty-seven years after 007 appeared on the big screen for the very first time, the release of Bond's latest loves and adventures in the final November of the twentieth century was anticipated with unprecedented excitement

The World Is Not Enough, from UIP/MGM, was released in Britain on 26 November 1999, but almost a year earlier the *Daily Telegraph*, no less, had carried a prominent quarter-page picture of bikini-clad, 26-year-old actress Denise Richards, for no other reason than that she was being tipped as the latest Bond girl. The movie was not even due to begin filming for another six weeks.

Four months later the same paper devoted a generous half page to the new movie under the banner headline 'JAMES BOND TURNS THE BIG GUNS ON MI6'. Four pictures accompanied the report, one showing a dramatic scene from the new movie being shot at Waterloo Pier; another of the Thames-side headquarters of MI6; and then smaller individual head shots of Pierce Brosnan and a 'shocked Janet Anderson'. The thrust of the feature was that the producers had been finding it difficult to obtain permission to shoot action sequences of speedboats on the Thames, showing MI6 headquarters in the background, until the then arts minister, Miss Anderson, stepped in to help. A high-level source commented: 'After all that Bond has done for Britain, it was the least we could do for Bond.'

The *Daily Mail* were on to the new Bond movie even earlier. More than a year ahead of the picture's general release, the popular tabloid had looked to movie bad girl Natasha Henstridge as a possible candidate for the girlie villainous role of Holly Christmas (Dr Christmas Jones, as it turned out) in the new film. Later, the press reported that a 15-foot helium airship being used in the new Bond film had gone missing after its cable broke at Pinewood Studios, allowing it to drift away. The *Daily Express* claimed that Desmond Llewelyn, killed in December 1999, who had played Q for the first time in *From Russia With Love* in 1963, would make his last appearance in the role in the new film. The *Sun*, meanwhile, claimed that Brosnan himself was becoming somewhat troublesome by insisting that established Hollywood star Sharon Stone be cast as the Bond bad girl in the new movie. And the *Sunday Times*, of all papers, suggested that antipodean rugby star Jonah Lomu, all eighteen stone-plus of him, was up for the part of Bond's latest adversary. True or false, right or wrong, when James Bond comes along the media bring out their big battalions in a feverish battle to muscle in on the act in order to boost their circulations.

When Pierce Brosnan hitched his star to James Bond just four years before, he might have been forgiven for thinking that the superhero's days were numbered. But it was the triumph of Brosnan himself, in *GoldenEye* and then *Tomorrow Never Dies*, which had breathed new life into the ageing super-spy. Those two films grossed a record-breaking $700 million at the box office, securing the foreseeable future of the world's most successful film franchise. At the same time it made Pierce Brosnan the most financially successful Bond of all time.

But how long can you continue to serve up the same old recipe? The public demands the impossible. They want more of the James Bond they know and love, but at the same time don't want to return home feeling they've seen it all before. So how do you make it different . . . but not too different? How do you make it better without jettisoning the key elements that make Bond what it is? Changes had to be subtle and well thought out, because, as Brosnan explained: 'It is impossible to keep adding bigger and bigger bangs.' In fact the then forty-five-year old actor's input was a measure of how the whole process had been made more demo-cratic. And there was definitely a feeling that Bond needed to be taken in a different direction.

Producers Michael G. Wilson and Barbara Broccoli were shrewd enough to know all this. So was Brosnan who, for reasons which were commercial, but also artistic, saw Bond's evolution as essen-tial. 'I don't just want to run around with a machine gun from start to finish,' he declared as the film began shooting. 'Having big, punchy set-pieces is a hallmark of the Bond films, but I also want to be tested as an actor and make my character more of a flesh-and-blood man.' Brosnan's views about how James Bond should project himself were certainly very much part of the carefully controlled evolutionary process. It would not have happened in Connery's day, when the actor was there simply to perform.

To direct the new and nineteenth official Bond adventure, Wilson and Broccoli brought in Michael Apted, the 55-year-old British-born director with some twenty-five movies to his credit. He was perhaps best known in the eighties for *Gorky Park*, a spy thriller from Martin Cruz's best-seller. The selection was surprising, because Apted, though a highly-respected figure in movie-making and a skilful creator of documentaries, had little, if any, experience in making all-action films. Nor had he done anything on the scale of a Bond movie before. But the key point was that Apted's views on how Bond should be on the eve of the twenty-first century coincided with those of the producers and with Brosnan himself. Seen as essential was the need to ground the action in a deeper, more substantial storyline, without sacrificing the Bond pyrotechnics. This was achieved through a better script, stronger characterizations of some of the supporting players and through the Bond girls having a more significant part to play, not just there as Bond's playthings.

Apted pointed out a further development. 'Women are central to the film, of course, but in a completely different way. We want to bring Bond up to date with a different attitude to women and we want women of a totally different type in this latest film.' The Bond girls would continue to be a vital element in the movie, but not merely as sexual foils. From this reasoning developed the idea of having, for the first time, a female cast as a serious, major villain.

As the world's favourite secret agent, 007 would now begin openly to show some occasional vulnerability, greater sophistication and subtlety and an increased sense of humanity. This was to be a new Bond to greet the new millennium, no longer impervious to pain or immune from self-doubt. The brutal self-glorification of sixties' Bond had to be buried for ever. And Pierce was by no means attracted to spending five months shooting an AK47 or dodging explosions. For both himself and for the future of James Bond, he wanted to do realistic scenes and have realistic relationships. The result would certify that these adjustments had been developed with skill, intelligence and sensitivity.

Brosnan agreed that the elegant lifestyle of Bond was all part of his charisma, as was the tongue-in-cheek humour. Those aspects had to be preserved, as did the powerful action sequences, the awe-inspiring set pieces, those glamorous and exotic locations, and the ability of our hero to triumph over evil whatever the odds. But over the years some of the essential elements to be found in Fleming's original stories had been obscured. Maybe James had become just a bit too superficial, too mechanical perhaps and too unfeeling.

As these fundamentals were still being thrashed out, and even before the British writing team of Neal Purvis and Robert Wade began beavering away on the script in early 1998, Wilson and Barbara Broccoli had set their date for total completion of the new $110 million (£70 million) production: an extremely optimistic mid November 1999. This allowed for a panicky shooting time of six months maximum, preferably five. It was a tough assignment, even with multiple film units sometimes working concurrently to a demanding schedule in a range of worldwide locations – snow-capped French Alps, Scottish castles, oil-pipelines in Turkey.

Barbara Broccoli was said to have been on a flight to Miami, watching a film about the Caspian Sea, when she first had the idea for *The World Is Not Enough*. With the collapse of the Soviet Union, Baku, the capital of the newly independent Muslim state of Azerbaijan, was now the centre of the world's new oil boom. Wrap a good story around that, with an archetypal Bond villain trying to control the world's oil supply for purely selfish reasons by blowing up competitive pipelines, and you have a challenge momentous enough for James Bond to tackle – but then only on the specific instructions of M!

Brosnan had not been entirely idle since packing away his Bond persona at the end of *Tomorrow Never Dies*. His schedules for *Grey Owl*, and then *The Thomas Crown Affair* were tightly packed together and *The World Is Not Enough* (said to have been taken from Ian Fleming's family motto) would be the third film he had worked on in little more than a year. And a Bond film, even going smoothly, is never the easiest of rides. As Michael Caine once astutely observed, when talking about Roger Moore in the role, 'Surely, nothing can compare with the pressure of being the new James Bond.' Pierce was by no means new at this point, of course, but the tensions associated with such a high-profile role hardly diminish when the stakes are so high and the audience is global. But, as Pierce revealed later: 'Producing *The Thomas Crown Affair* gave me a certain confidence.'

There was an optimistic air about the place as the new picture began shooting on Monday, 11 January 1999, because the Bond team was back at Pinewood Studios, its spiritual home, for the first time in ten years. The sound stage there is the biggest in the country, and before shooting began, the vast outdoor water tank that measures 600 by 400 feet had been enclosed with 60-feet-high walls in order to re-create a caviar factory perched on walkways over the Caspian Sea. It would be the first time that Brosnan had worked at Pinewood, but the place retained a special significance for him. First, he had been a special kind of visitor there almost twenty years before when *For Your Eyes Only* was being shot, accompanying his then girlfriend Cassandra Harris who, of course, had a small part in the movie. And it was also at Pinewood five years later that he would have made his debut as James Bond in *The Living Daylights*, had not his *Remington Steele* contract cruelly intervened.

Back together in front of the cameras were Dame Judi Dench (M); Desmond Llewelyn (the testy, gadget supremo Q), making his seventeenth appearance alongside James; and Samantha Bond (the ever-faithful Miss Moneypenny). But there were many new faces too.

Glamorous French actress Sophie Marceau was significantly the first ever woman to be cast in the role of a serious Bond villain. The 33-year-old plays the beautiful and mysterious Elektra King, daughter of assassinated oil tycoon Sir Robert King, and she keeps us guessing for some time about which side she is really on. Although Marceau was a 'veteran' of almost a score of movies and enjoyed a huge following in France, it was not until she played Princess Isabelle in the Mel Gibson medieval epic *Braveheart* in 1995 that she became widely known. She explained her surprise at being chosen for this major role in a James Bond movie: 'They [the producers and Michael Apted] had seen me playing a nineteenth-century Swiss governess in *Firelight* and asked to see me when I was in England. I must have done something right because they offered me the role, but quite how they got from *Firelight* to Elektra is bizarre.' She admitted that she hadn't seen a Bond film since she was thirteen, some twenty years ago.

In this latest 007 epic the Paris-born beauty demonstrates just how well she can act and, despite being the nefarious super-villain – calm, ice-cool and wicked – she is at the same time far too sexy and accessible to be ignored by Bond, even allowing for his own personality make-over. She is a more enigmatic woman than any previous Bond female, but even so it comes as no surprise when she and James get together between the sheets; but the die is irrevocably cast when she blames James for the death of her father knowing she was herself cynically responsible. Her duplicity is complete when she teams up with the villainous Renard (Robert Carlyle), a Bosnian terrorist with a bullet lodged in his brain that makes him impervious to pain, and becomes a deadly foe of Bond. But Elektra never quite loses her feelings for 007. When she is unable to persuade him to join forces with her and all seems to be lost, she says with sad resignation: 'I could've given you the world'; to which, like a man who could really have felt something for her, he replies: 'The world is not enough.' While making the film Sophie rented a house in Kensington with Polish director Andrzej Zulawski, the 57-year-old father of her son Vincent, and somehow managed to find enough spare time occasionally to go bargain-hunting in Portobello Road.

Incidentally, being cast in a James Bond movie was an international breakthrough at the highest level for Robert Carlyle, even allowing for his impact as the psycho in *Trainspotting* and the hapless, sympathetic character in the massive hit *The Full Monty*.

But Bond means girls, of course, and Denise Richards and Maria

187

Grazia Cucinotta complete the team for *The World Is Not Enough*. The winsome Richards emerges as the sexiest nuclear weapons expert there has ever been, or is ever likely to be, in the all-action role of Dr Christmas Jones, who shows her expertise by defusing a nuclear bomb. Simply working on a Bond movie for the first time was nerve-racking, at the beginning anyway, particularly as she accompanies 007 on a series of active escapades. But she asked the more experienced Pierce for his advice on how best to handle some of her physically demanding scenes. 'He would show me how to fall properly without injury and suggest when protective clothing and pads were necessary,' she explained. 'Having done two earlier Bond movies he had coped with a lot of action scenes and knew how to go about things.'

As with Marceau, this part was a big leg-up for Richards, an emerging star from a Chicago suburb whose pedigree included *Starship Troopers*, *Wild Things* and, most recent of all, *Drop Dead Gorgeous*. She did not hesitate when offered the role. 'The films are classics and to be part of history is fabulous,' she explained. In the picture she is a devoted ally of Bond and the target of one of 007's characteristic verbal innuendos, which had begun to crop up with tiresome regularity during Roger Moore's days, but had been toned down since. As *Total Film* noted at the time: 'Brosnan turns to orgasm-shuddering Richards and mugs: "I thought Christmas came only once a year." ' It was an appropriate scene with which to end the movie and in the finest tradition of Bond. But on the whole, the new feminist formula was well maintained during the movie, and Richards was happy that her character had more depth than most of the previous Bond girls. 'It's more than running around and hanging on to Bond's arm,' she revealed ahead of the picture's release. The 27-year-old Denise Richards would spend one climactic scene with Brosnan climbing into a submarine that fills up with water – and was reported to be getting paid £1 million for her trouble. Certainly both she and Sophie Marceau had their own agendas and avoided caricature.

The smouldering dark sensuality of Sicilian-born Maria Grazia Cucinotta helped her to stand out in her sinister role as the 'Cigar Girl'. Such is the international impact of the Bond–Brosnan combination that when the Sicilians discovered she was in the movie, Maria said, 'it was like I'd won an Oscar'. She added enthusiastically: 'I'm a killer in the picture, a soldier for hire and I work for Robert Carlyle (Renard) . . . he's my boss.' Then dejectedly: 'My job is to try to kill Bond, but I'm the only girl in the movie who doesn't get to kiss him.' Not surprising really, since her exit from the movie comes even before the opening titles are completed. On the other hand, brevity of appearance need not preclude a romantic encounter. Serena Scott Thomas, who plays Dr Molly Warmflash in *The World Is Not Enough*, shares with Bond what is by far the sexiest scene in the entire picture – and by far the briefest. However, Cucinotta seemed happy enough just working with Brosnan. 'Pierce is wonderful, he made me laugh and I felt really comfortable with him,' she declared. 'For me he is the best super-spy of the franchise.'

It appeared obvious from this latest Bond that Brosnan was continuing to mature in the part, helped, it appears, by what he considered to be a better film. 'It is more coherent than *Tomorrow Never Dies* and I am more confident and assured with myself,' he explained. 'Michael Apted is a great director, very good on stuff like character and story, though he probably wasn't an obvious choice for a Bond movie. But the new film has character and wit, plenty of drama and tells a good story.' It was more spectacular and altogether more realistic than previous Bonds. This gave Brosnan an opportunity to go deeper into the role.

Pierce was reported to have sat in on all the script meetings and encouraged to give his comments; the idea was to give 007 more light and shade. Pierce explained: 'For the first time there is a sense of doubt in the Bond character, a feeling that he might be in over his head, maybe.' For one thing, Bond feels somehow at fault over the demise of oil tycoon Sir Robert King, so he instinctively goes to protect King's daughter Elektra. Only later and after becoming emotionally involved with her, does he realize that the person he considered to be responsible is not the culprit after all. 'It all leads to exciting scenes with nuance and subtext,' Pierce explained.

His somewhat underplayed representation, the sense of inner control and strength, gave 007 a greater conviction without losing any of the special 'whimsical' charm that is inextricably linked to Bond. It certainly impressed Carlyle, an actor not normally much given to verbal extravagances. A dedicated Connery man, Carlyle none the less gained an enormous admiration for Brosnan's work after appearing in *The World Is Not Enough*. He felt the Irishman had brought Bond back to life. 'Pierce has set fire to the whole thing again,' he explained. 'He's a star. He has a quality few actors have and there's a charisma about him. Pierce has found his strength as Bond; it just emerges from him naturally.' More than one independent commentator picked up on how much more assured Brosnan appeared in the role in his latest Bond outing. 'The smoothest spy in history,' was one independent accolade.

Brosnan certainly takes the part seriously, even though he had played the character twice before. He takes nothing for granted. His research is said to be thorough, and to remind himself of where it all came from, he will periodically re-read some of Ian Fleming's original stories. As Bond, he apparently makes a conscious effort to eliminate or disguise his slight Irish accent; it is part of the determination to keep even small details authentic. His colleagues and co-stars confirm how assiduously he will work to get things right. In his understated way, he told television talkshow host Clive Anderson: 'You have to respect the role.' And with the quiet assurance which has become his hallmark, he told Jonathan Ross: 'I knew what I wanted to do . . . I knew what I didn't want to do.'

Even before its release it seemed that Brosnan had secured the role for at least one more outing, should he want to take it. Michael Wilson said at the end of shooting: 'I think he's game for another one, certainly we are.' Shortly after, Pierce confirmed on British television that there was an option for him to do a fourth Bond, that he had been asked to do it and he had accepted. 'After that, who knows?' he said, smiling.

Seeing British actor Robbie Coltrane in the cast could have taken some Bond fanatics by surprise, but, then again, should not have done. For director Apted said he had been impressed by him in *GoldenEye* and wanted him back in a beefed-up part as Valentin Zukovsky, a Russian gangster, a former KGB agent turned supplier to terrorists. A genuine surprise, however, was the casting of funny man John Cleese as R, the new assistant to gadget-freak Q. Rumour had it that Cleese would take over from Llewelyn in the next Bond movie, but Q would have none of it. 'Not the next one,' said the 85-year-old veteran of seventeen Bond movies. But fate removed all doubts when the lovable actor was tragically killed on 19 December 1999, only shortly after the release of *The World Is Not Enough*. He was involved in a car accident in east Sussex after attending a book-signing session of *Q: The Biography of Desmond Llewelyn*.

With eighteen full-blooded official Bond stories already in the can, and the requirement to make this the best yet, where do you look for the latest and greatest plot? This time around the writers found it in a global power struggle, with the world's oil supplies in jeopardy. Elektra's father is a very powerful man and the owner of oil refineries around the world. His murder at the beginning of the film means that Elektra inherits his huge business, making her extremely rich and powerful. Bond is sent to investigate his murder and to protect his daughter, whom the authorities now feel could be in extreme danger. That is just the start, and there are many layers in this most subtle and complex addition to the genre.

The battle strikes at the heart of world espionage when a major explosion erupts inside the MI6 building. Bond charges in to defuse this grave situation. His heroics are aided and abetted by nuclear scientist Christmas Jones (the nubile Richards) as they travel to Istanbul, where a former enemy becomes an influential ally prior to the final confrontation in a nuclear submarine. Much of the film would be shot in London, but those essential far-flung and sometimes exotic locations, a Bond trademark, would this time include: Switzerland, for a spectacular ski-chase sequence made doubly difficult because of recent heavy snowfalls and avalanches; Spain; the snow-capped peaks of the French Alps; Scottish castles; and the oil-rich areas of Turkey and Azerbaijan.

But Bond tradition is most obviously maintained by what proves to be the longest, most ambitious pre-credit action sequence in the entire history of James Bond movies, the stunning speedboat chase on the Thames, from MI6 headquarters to the Millennium Dome. A massive explosion has ripped out part of the MI6 building, and the villainous Cigar Girl, perpetrator of the deed, makes her dramatic escape in the 42-foot-long, twin-engined, fully-armed Sunseeker speedboat. Bond gives chase in a jet boat borrowed from Q, which blasts out of the now gaping hole in the MI6 building, flying through the air before thumping down on the water at a speed approaching 40 knots.

For some fourteen minutes the frantic, high-speed chase continues, with Bond managing to evade a continuous fusillade of fire power from the Cigar Girl. During the pursuit Brosnan's hurtling boat leaves the river and crashes through a smart, glitzy riverside restaurant and wedding marquee (the former in reality an eighteenth-century wharf-side building on a desolate outpost of Docklands), before zooming back on to the Thames again. Powerboat racer and stunt girl Sarah Donohue, who did many of the high-speed manoeuvres on the Thames, had broken both arms, a wrist and her jaw while racing in Venice in August, and had been

192

engaged to abseil down the face of the Trocadero in London to mark the opening of its James Bond museum.

The World Is Not Enough's spectacular opening sequences, some of which cost a staggering $1 million a minute to film, the most expensive single shoot in 007 history, took thirty-four days to complete. It was for his work on this Thames scene particularly that Brosnan won the admiration of stunt coordinator Simon Crane and second-unit director Vic Armstrong, both of whom had worked on *Titanic* and *Saving Private Ryan*. Said Armstrong: 'He was superb, jumping the waves at 60 to 65 m.p.h., getting hit in the face; it's like a sledgehammer when water whacks you at that speed.'

Brosnan insisted on getting fully involved in as many of the remarkable stunts as possible and impressed the stunt team with his ability to control high-speed boats. It was during the shooting of this scene that he came perilously close to hitting the buttress of Lambeth Bridge. 'This was because I was so preoccupied with keeping the House of Commons in shot,' he explained. But by this time, it appears that MPs had become well accustomed to seeing Brosnan and other members of the cast racing speedboats along the Thames in front of the Houses of Parliament.

According to Crane, the most spectacular stunt and the most dangerous ever seen on the Thames is when Bond's boat leaps over his assailant's craft, the jet thrusters rotating the boat through 360 degrees in a manoeuvre known as a barrel roll. It was rehearsed seventeen times on land before the scene moved to the water, where, astonishingly, the very first attempt was a totally successful wrap. If that's not breathtaking enough, add a succession of explosions, plenty of automatic gunfire, and a spectacular balloon escape that doesn't work out.

The sequence ends in equally dramatic fashion. As Bond closes in on Cigar Girl, she scrambles into the basket of a hot-air balloon to make her escape, but 007 clutches at a trailing rope and hangs on. She continues to fire at him as he begins to climb steadily up the rope. Once she sees the game is up, she fires her automatic into the balloon. There is an enormous explosion, she is presumably killed and Bond is thrown high and wide and ends up landing on the roof of the Millennium Dome – still in control, scarcely out of breath and no permanent damage done.

This latest Bond bash elevates greed, revenge and attempted world domination to even greater heights of ruthlessness. Bilbao, Spain, on the top floor of the Guggenheim Museum, is where the film opens, in heart-stopping style. After a tussle James uses a tied-up human baddie (alive and kicking) as a counter-balance as, holding securely to the other end of the rope, he swings out of the open window before making his escape by abseiling down to ground level and casually walking away. All the stunts were professionally co-ordinated, one of the scariest being the scene of a massive avalanche in the Caucasus mountains. Another revolved around stopping a potential nuclear explosion in a vast circular oil pipeline in Turkey. Reminded of the scene, Pierce explained: 'The huge fire-ball is hurtling after us and there is only one chance of survival.' He and Sophie Marceau make it to safety, of course, but in reality the crew had a fully manned fire truck and ambulance standing by, just in case.

In total a 500-strong crew from Eon Productions was involved in making the picture; two hundred of them descended on Trinity Buoy Wharf for a whole month to film the sensational opening scenes. More than 1,000 people were said to be employed during the six months the film was in production. And of course, the release of the movie during the final build-up of Millennium fever provided a unique topicality, with the Dome at Greenwich becoming a star in its own right.

The World Is Not Enough, maintains tradition with an extraordinary assortment of special gadgets. The most spectacular perhaps belongs to Bond's enemies, being a hybrid of a snowmobile and a parachute, called a parahawk, and used during the ambush scene on the Caucasus mountains in Central Asia. At the other end of the scale are the somewhat farcical killer bagpipes that fire bullets or jets of flame instead of making music, and which are made ready for use after MI6 has relocated to Scotland after the terrorist attack on its London HQ. Also included in this latest assortment are a hand-held computer weighing less than nine ounces; pairs of glasses that can emit a blinding flash of light or a jet of tear gas; a ski-jacket which is also an air-bag; Bond's special X-ray glasses that allow him to see through clothing; and of course his essential Omega wristwatch. This time it incorporates a miniature grappling hook with 50 feet of high-tensile retractable micro-filament wire. There is also a credit card that he can use for lock-picking and, of course, 007's essential car, the very latest BMW Z8, titanium-armoured with missiles in its headlamps and a snooper beam to pick up distant conversations. The idea of the helicopter equipped with rapidly revolving saw blades – used at one stage to slice a car in two – was said to have come from a Laurel and Hardy movie.

A James Bond movie is always an energy-sapping, if exhilarating, experience, so Brosnan prepared for the rigours ahead with regular weight-training sessions under the guidance of his personal trainer Simon Waterson. He needed to be fit, as anyone could attest who saw him emerge soaked and physically drained from repeated scalings of the walls of a crashed submarine stuck vertically at the bottom of the Caspian Sea – even when enacted on Pinewood's famous large sound stage. This represents the exciting climax to the film, as Bond and Christmas, along with villain Renard, battle to stay alive and gain the upper hand in a Russian submarine's nuclear reactor room as it sinks to the bed of the Caspian Sea and starts to flood.

It is extraordinary that a project so immense and complex was completed largely without unforeseen difficulties and within the allotted five- to six-months' schedule, though there were some behind-the-scene anxieties. Not unusually with a project of this kind, the scripts at times were still being worked on much too close to the shooting schedule, the story-writing process by this time having been helped along by Bruce Feirstein. For some time, moreover, a potent fear of litigation hung over the proceedings like a black cloud. Wilson and Barbara Broccoli were engaged in a long-running lawsuit to prevent Sony from launching a rival Bond series, and the project was halfway through the shooting before the dispute was settled satisfactorily in favour of MGM, who finance the Eon Productions Bond projects.

A prodigious volume of publicity was generated in the two or three weeks prior to the movie's British release, and anticipation was running at an all-time high, even for a Bond film. It was hailed as the biggest and best Bond movie of all time. The *Sunday Times* produced a 'special Bond collectors' issue' magazine, which offered the lucky winners to a competition 'the ultimate James Bond experience', including tickets for the European charity premiere of the new film and an invitation to the star-studded party afterwards; a trip to Istanbul for a winner and guest, with a stay at the Bosphorus Hotel; a cruise; a visit to Scotland to visit some of the film's location sites, followed by a journey to London to stay at the Mandarin Oriental Hyde Park and ride up the Thames in the Sunseeker speedboat featured in the film.

Other sources offered other attractions, like a Club Med skiing holiday in the French mountain resort of Chamonix, where some of the Bond sequences were filmed. Another linked promotion dangled a 'fabulous 007-style weekend in London, driving in fast cars and flying in helicopters.' Among a whole raft of subsidiary prizes with links to the new movie were a Sony PlayStation with a new Bond game and soundtrack albums from the film. For just two tokens from *The Times*, readers were rewarded with a free giant-size Bond poster. The *Daily Express* climbed aboard with a free video-for-tokens scheme.

Brosnan did his share of promotion work, stepping out of his normally private lifestyle to co-operate in his usual charming style with a series of media interviews. He talked about changes in James Bond over the years and his own experiences in the role. 'I've figured out what I'm doing, finally.' When asked the hoary old question of whether he would do another Bond film, his reply was equally patient and modest: 'I'd like to do one more,' he said, and then, with that disarming mannerism of fingers pointing to the mouth and eye, 'I think I've got the hang of it now.'

Any movie so hugely hyped is certain to be carefully scrutinized by the critics, and here and there it was given a lukewarm reception. London *Evening Standard*'s veteran film critic, Alexander Walker, suggested he was 'shaken, but not moved' by it all, though he added: 'This adventure will see Bond nicely into the Millennium.' Few critics however would seriously quarrel with *Daily Telegraph* reporter Nigel Reynolds' assessment of Brosnan's performance: 'In the bar-room game of who is the best Bond of all time, Brosnan's imperiously cool performance – manly and definitely not politically correct New Man – should confirm him among the best.' And in general the film opened to wide acclaim and enthusiasm. Clayton Hickman in *Film Review* bordered on the ecstatic with: 'It's got absolutely everything. And it's got it all spot on.' And Brosnan? 'He is an absolute revelation here . . . and imbues the character with an emotional intensity that recalls Timothy Dalton's portrayal, though with a sheen and charisma that brings Connery's early outings to mind.' One critic was even moved to speculate that Brosnan 'might just be the best 007 of them all.' Another said he brought 'intelligence and wit, together with a lightness, to the role.'

The World Is Not Enough had its glittering world premiere in Hollywood on 9 November 1999. The film zoomed to the top of the charts in the United States and broke box-office records there by taking some $45 million (£23.3 million) in its opening weekend. Brosnan attended the star-studded occasion with Keely Shaye-Smith, along with Denise Richards and Maria Grazia Cucinotta. The picture opened in Britain on 26 November 1999, and was preceded by a British and European charity premiere in London four days earlier. Leicester Square was tightly packed with fans keen to catch a glimpse of all the big stars, but it was a glamorous Keely, on Brosnan's arm, who just might have stolen the show by wearing a £3.5 million diamond necklace.

It was an occasion when the press took every advantage to quiz Brosnan about Bond in general and his possible future in the role. Marceau said her role was very important and that she and Pierce 'matched very well'. Brosnan did not accept that he played a softer Bond, this third time around. 'It's the same Bond in many ways, but I just wanted to make the character a bit more accessible,' he explained. Then, maybe just a little testily: 'It is my interpretation whether you like it or not.' Later he elaborated: 'I think Bond has still a lot of mileage in him and I love playing the guy; he's great fun and I've tried to stamp him with my own personality.'

Anyone who might just be worried about Bond's future after *The World Is Not Enough*, need have no fear, for as tradition now dictates, the closing message gave the assurance that ... James Bond will return. And that means, barring accidents, so too will Pierce Brosnan.

15

The Man with the Golden Touch

OWEN MILES HAS BEEN SELLING CYCLES successfully in the town of Street in Somerset for more than fifteen years. The particular day in question, early October 1999, was turning out to be very much an average sort of day. Or so he thought. It was just after 12 noon, the morning trade was over and the afternoon customers had yet to start filtering in. The late-summer sun had managed to escape the clouds; the shop was quiet; it was all very pleasant. Owen was about to take a well-earned breather when the shop-door opened and a couple of men walked in.

'Hello,' said the older man, pleasantly. 'I'm Pierce Brosnan. I've just called in to introduce myself.' He was wearing sunglasses and casually dressed in T-shirt, jeans and cardigan. The younger man was introduced as Pierce's son Christopher. But what were they doing in Street? More specifically, what were they doing in Owen Miles's cycle shop? Even more to the point: why didn't Owen collapse in a heap on the spot from total surprise and astonishment?

First, Brosnan's sixteen-year-old son Sean was, at the time, a pupil at nearby Millfield School, following in the family tradition established when Cassie had been alive, when both Charlotte and

Christopher had spent four years there. Secondly, Pierce and Christopher had stayed in the Somerset town over the weekend at the Bear Hotel while visiting Sean for his birthday and arranging to buy a bicycle for him to celebrate the occasion. And the reason Owen Miles was not totally bowled over was because Pierce's personal secretary had earlier telephoned long-distance from Tokyo to set up the purchase.

'All the same, it was a bit unexpected; but I was thrilled about it and most impressed,' said Owen. 'He didn't really have to go to all that trouble of coming in to introduce himself, because all the arrangements were going through okay. It was a really nice gesture for someone in his position. He didn't just rush in and rush out and in a way it was lucky there was no one in the shop at the time, or I might have had to keep him waiting. He seemed a very nice person, friendly and very ordinary and gave no impression of being anyone special.'

Owen said that they were in the shop for about ten minutes and then politely and quietly left, thanking him for attending to everything. Having just departed, Christopher apparently nipped back into the shop to ask Owen if he could tell him where the nearest public telephone was, since they wanted to make a call for their car and driver to pick them up. Owen explained: 'I said to Christopher why didn't he use my shop phone since it would be much easier. So that's what he did, thanked me again and left to wait with his father outside for the car to arrive.' It transpired that on the way to Owen's shop Pierce and Christopher had walked the length of the town's High Street and nobody had recognized them.

But there was one other incident of note from the visit. Knowing how awkward such a request can be for celebrities, Owen tentatively produced a camera and asked Pierce if he would mind having a picture taken. 'I was surprised,' said Owen. 'He said certainly, it was no problem and explained that as Christopher was good with cameras, why didn't he take the picture.' That's how

Owen Miles, cycle retailer from Street, came to have his picture taken with the internationally famous James Bond. Something special for the family album.

Those who know Pierce Brosnan will not be surprised by the story. Despite his fame and fortune, he is said to be considerate, helpful, and genuinely friendly. It was significant too that he introduced Christopher as his son. For when *GoldenEye* was released a few years before and a journalist asked him, 'I understand you've been working with your stepson on this film?' Brosnan hesitated for a moment, then responded quietly: 'Yes, Christopher . . . but I prefer to use the word son.' He also took the chance to pre-empt the subtle implication behind the question: 'When I went off to Papua New Guinea to play Robinson Crusoe [his last commitment before taking over as James Bond] I got Christopher a job on the film, and I got him a job on *GoldenEye* too. But the buck stops here. The next job he gets himself.' In fact Christopher had made his own decision to find some kind of career in films and had studied seriously at New York University Film School. It was only then, after Christopher had made the decision independently, that he received full support and encouragement from his father. Christopher was twenty-two when he worked on *GoldenEye* – 'still a boy,' said Pierce, 'but it's good to see him work his ass off on a big picture with a highly-trained crew like this'.

Pierce Brosnan continues to be every inch the family man. He is deeply involved with everyone close to him, but since Charlotte and Christopher have now grown into full-blown adults with largely independent lives of their own, his attention has focused more on Sean and now, of course, Dylan Thomas. Just a few years ago he told a reporter proudly: 'My daughter Charlotte is an actress too, as beautiful as her mother and with that same sense of humour.' Her first job was in Los Angeles in *NYPD Blue* but aged twenty-eight (in 1999), she is now a mother herself and carries the distinction of making Bond a grandfather for the first time. But grinning broadly, Pierce told the London *Evening Standard*'s Marianne Gray: 'But I still have my own teeth and hair.' Yet despite the love and close feelings he has for his own family, he appears not to have completely forgiven his father for moving out when Pierce was so young. Tom Brosnan died in the summer of 1988, but according to reports, Pierce did not go to the funeral, though that may have been because film commitments prevented it. He continues to be close to his mother, sixty-nine years old in 2000.

One anecdote from the making of *The World Is Not Enough* indicates his generally equable disposition. He seems to have a knack for making people close to him feel comfortable. The film used lots of extras, and at one point when a scene had been shot and the excitement had calmed down, a couple of women from Essex who had been working as extras found themselves standing close to Brosnan. After some time, and conquering her fear, one of the women approached him: 'Can we have a photograph?' she asked tentatively. There came back a smile, a brief pause, and then: 'I thought you'd never ask.' As an observer remarked at the time: 'He has great style and charm.'

Being at the top in the tough world of movie-making, Pierce Brosnan is hardly likely to be a saint; and to have come through the tough periods and punishing disappointments, not to mention the loss of a much loved wife so early in life, suggests an inner steel not wholly compatible with his easy-going persona. But none the less he does leave the impression of a down-to-earth humanity, despite all his popularity and fame.

For many years the Omega watch company has been closely linked with Bond movies. While shooting a new advertisement for the watches in June 1999 Brosnan heard that freelance photographer Ian West, who was working on the assignment, was grumbling about having to turn out on his birthday. When the shoot ended, Brosnan caught up with West and asked him if it really was his birthday. West said yes, and Brosnan was said to have whipped off his own watch (valued at more than £1,000 and engraved 'The World Is Not Enough') and handed it over to West. 'Happy birthday,' he said with a smile, before walking away.

The chance meeting with Keely Shaye-Smith proved to be a key turning-point in Pierce Brosnan's life. After Cassie's death he admitted to feeling like only half a person. 'It was painful and frightening and you have to rediscover yourself,' he explained. As a former model, Keely was already something of a public figure when they met, having been involved in the promotion of the Estee Lauder organic cruelty-free cosmetic range, and their mutual affection came naturally from the start. It wasn't long before he was proudly proclaiming that she had become 'part of my life'. He took her to Ireland, where they swam with the dolphins; and indeed almost from the beginning of their relationship he became closely involved with her environmental activities.

While Bond has played a positive and dominant role in recent years, Brosnan works hard at not letting it monopolize his film work. He and his business partner appear to have a balanced approach to the development of their production company, Irish Dream Time. Pierce certainly wants to continue to make films that not only satisfy his creative urge, but which incorporate more profound themes and ideas – films which, as he put it, have a heart and need to be told.

In recent years Brosnan has become an effective and articulate advocate for the health concerns of women. He served as the Ambassador for Women's Health Issues for the Permanent Charities Committee of the Entertainment Industries, and in that capacity has addressed key members of the United States Congress about ovarian cancer, the disease that claimed the life of Cassandra. Since then he has helped to raise more than £3 million for women's health research.

He is strongly involved in Gilda's Club, which provides a

meeting place for cancer sufferers, their friends and family, and also offers support groups, lectures, workshops and social events. As Pierce explained: 'The club takes its name from Gilda Radner, who was a good friend of my late wife Cassie and they were both fighting ovarian cancer at around the same time. They were strong, powerful women yet they both lost the fight, Gilda in 1989 and Cassie in 1991.' It was Gene Wilder, Gilda's husband, who came up with the idea of Gilda's Club, and it first saw the light of day in the United States. It is a place where sufferers can go and talk and have therapy individually or in a group, completely free.

While Pierce has coped with the private anguish of Cassie's death with commendable bravery, it is clear that building a new life for himself has not cancelled out the pain of those years. It has not been easy. In those dreadful days following her death, when the children were younger and they were attempting to recover from their grief, both together and individually, he felt it important not to show his sense of despair. The dignity and courage which Cassie herself had shown during their darkest days served as his own model of behaviour. He once told *OK* magazine that he tries not to take anything for granted any more, taking each day as a gift to be cherished and enjoyed.

When Gilda's Club asked him to become their patron, he immediately agreed, despite the obvious pressures on his time. He said he was proud to be involved with the charity and honoured to be patron. A prestigious dinner at a private club in London's Portman Square, which Pierce attended with Keely, marked his inauguration as patron. He said he was happy to be in a position where he could raise awareness of the need for the kind of support Gilda's Club offers. He said with obvious sincerity and feeling: 'Gilda's Club is a great sanctuary. When one person gets cancer the whole family suffers.' Until Pierce came along the London club had plenty of women helping out, but not many men. To change this is vital, because, as a spokesperson for the club pointed out, Gilda's Club isn't just about women, it's about families and husbands, young men and old. In this respect Brosnan said he was delighted at the higher profile his success as James Bond had brought. 'Without that I would not be able to be nearly as useful in raising public awareness of this vital charity,' he explained.

The man who brought new life to Bond now lives with wife Keely, their young sons Dylan and Paris Beckett and four dogs in a secluded Canyon home in Malibu's exotic Paradise Cove, with Sean still based there and Charlotte and Christopher visiting from time to time. The couple also have a house in north London. Malibu is said to be home to more millionaires than any other town of comparable size on earth. With its sweeping beaches and beautiful coastline, it is the place to live if you are a megastar. Ironically, it doesn't always enjoy the best of weather, and it is not unusual for the Pacific Coast Highway, the main road into the beach city, to be closed because of heavy flooding. When that happens you stay at home or face a fifty-mile detour. The place has lived through rock- and mud-slides, tidal waves, fires and home-threatening floods. The emergency services coordinator for Los Angeles once described Malibu as the disaster capital of the world. 'It's the price you pay for living in paradise' has become an accepted slogan of the town. And it's a price most residents are happy to pay.

Brosnan can testify to the hazards. He was forced into buying his present home when his previous one virtually collapsed when caught in the middle of storms, mud-slides and floods. 'We just had to pull as much as we could out of the house and store it,' he explained. 'It's a bit scary, a natural disaster, and you don't just stand there and try to fight it.' He said he flung the important things he could salvage into the car and away he went. The wrecked house stood abandoned for some time before being sold recently for land value only.

In many respects Pierce Brosnan has resisted the

Americanization of his life, although he has now lived in the United States much longer than he has in Britain. There appears to be little evidence that he has done this as some bull-headed point of principle, staunchly defending his European heritage. Indeed it must be difficult to live for long in a place like Malibu without embracing much of the easy-going sunny Californian lifestyle. For this reason, too, it is not surprising that the quiet, modulated voice now carries more than a tinge of American inflection, though one can still easily pick up on his Anglo-Irish heritage.

His physical workout is a habit he picked up in the States; he absorbed it into his daily routine after preparing for his role as James Bond. It is a tough regime that Pierce insists is as good for the mind as it is for his body. He pumps iron, jogs and from time to time, particularly when Sean and he are home together, even does a bit of kick-boxing, riding, hang-gliding and swimming.

Once Pierce and Keely began living together, they could no longer pretend it was just a mild flirtation. So how about marriage? No rush, said Pierce repeatedly, refusing to be drawn. Even as recently as July 1999, when an interviewer asked the question again, the response was non-committal. 'Who knows what's around the corner?' he responded. He said that he and Keely were friends and lovers. Then added: 'Beyond that I can't say.' But the prospect continued to intrigue the press, particularly since it had been claimed that, despite Cassie's wish that he should find happiness in remarriage, he had once vowed never to do so.

Editors weren't prepared to bury the story. Here were two people with extremely high media profiles – he as James Bond and she as an environmental journalist whose early television work in the United States was well known. The love and devotion that Pierce and Cassandra had shared gave the story of the new relationship a poignant angle. For Brosnan came with a good deal of baggage. 'Cassie's spirit lives on in the children ... it's a magical thing,' he explained when interviewed as recently as mid 1999. Keely had certainly picked a hard act to follow, to the extent that she was step-ping into Cassie's shoes. What if Cassie had lived? When asked very recently if he still thought about his late wife, Pierce replied: 'All the time. Her energy didn't disappear just because she's dead. She's with the children and me, and with Keely and me in our new life.' He read-ily, if indirectly, acknowledged the unconventional situation in which they both found themselves. 'Keely's weathered a lot . . . we've weath-ered a lot together' – which might just be the key to the strength of their love. He later said that quite early on in their relationship he knew that Keely was someone he wanted to be with always.

It is probably this very sincerity that was to heighten the wide-spread speculation about their possible marriage. Pierce must have lost count of the number of times he explained to the press that marriage was not on the immediate agenda. After the success of *The Thomas Crown Affair* the 46-year-old Pierce and 33-year-old Keely, along with two-year-old Dylan, spent a short holiday in Italy, and were photographed by *Hello* magazine, mingling with tourists and generally enjoying relaxing on an informal family holi-day. It was a wonderful respite from the hectic life on a film-set, explained Pierce – a life that gave him too little time to spend with Keely and Dylan, although they had made a few visits to the studio to see him working on *Thomas Crown*.

Then, four months later, while Keely and Pierce were in Santa Monica, California, helping to publicize a campaign to save the grey whale, Keely was seen wearing a diamond-encrusted ring on her engagement finger. Journalists were convinced it had not been there a few days before during a press conference that the couple had attended. When challenged, Keely said that Pierce had asked her 'only recently' and, to further questioning, she responded with a smile: 'Yes, I'm very happy, thank you.' Then, in 2000, after finally setting the date for his marriage to Keely Shaye-Smith, the wedding was put on hold when his son, Sean, unexpectedly suffered complications following a horrific car crash.

Some months before, when asked about how he would be celebrating the millennium, Pierce admitted that he had received many invitations to big show-business parties, but that he had decided to stay at home for a quiet family celebration. 'There'll be a few bottles of champagne around and I will be with Keely and the whole family, Charlotte, Chris, Sean and my little son Dylan.'

Perhaps through the harsh experience of life itself, rather than natural inclination, Pierce Brendan Brosnan is not inclined to look too far into the future, but it is a future surely in which James Bond will figure prominently. The prodigious worldwide impact of *The World Is Not Enough* confirmed Brosnan's pulling power as a movie actor the public want to see. Through Bond, Brosnan has become ubiquitous, because the two are currently inseparable, and Bond, aka Brosnan, now touches life at so many different points and levels. The influence is immense and stretches round the world.

Even British royalty was not to be left out. Pierce met Prince Charles at the premiere of *GoldenEye*, and when Prince Edward was looking to boost the fortunes of his television company he turned to 007. He put forward an idea to make a multi-million pound series based on the life of James Bond. There would have been a pilot show ahead of the series and this, if successful, would be followed by twenty-two episodes costing in excess of £1 million. An additional idea was for a documentary about the making of the then latest Bond movie, *The World Is Not Enough*. Edward, Earl of Wessex, travelled to Hollywood to pitch his ideas to film company executives in person, but Barbara Broccoli and Michael Wilson were said to have turned down the idea, mainly on the basis that a television series might detract from Bond's triumphs on the big screen, and that Bond was not really in need of the boost of a documentary.

When in Britain television's *News at Ten* was switched to later in the evening against an uproar from viewers, ITN pulled out all the stops to prevent viewers from defecting in their thousands to the 'other side' with a specially trumpeted, high-profile screening of *GoldenEye*. The ubiquity of Bond cannot be denied. Author Phillip Knightley in his book *Philby: KGB-master spy*, published by André Deutsch in 1988, quoted Philby's comments on Allen Dulles (Director of CIA, 1953–61) – 'A touch of (Richard) Hannay perhaps; definitely not Bond (detestable fellow!).'

Brosnan is adamant, however, that there is more to him than Bond alone. After the success of *The Thomas Crown Affair*, there was talk of Brosnan, Russo and McTiernan reconvening to discuss the possibilities of a remake of King Vidor's *The Fountainhead*. The film, originally released in 1949, was described by one critic as being full of Freudian symbols and expressionist techniques; in the remake, Brosnan and Russo would take over the parts played by Gary Cooper and Patricia Neal. It is not likely to secure the widespread appeal of Bond, but sounds like an intriguing project.

Meantime, after his enormous success as Bond and his advancing reputation in other, varied roles, Brosnan was heavily in demand after *The World Is Not Enough*. It is perhaps typical of the man that he turned down all offers, determined instead to spend some quality time with Keely and his family at their main Malibu home. By early summer 2000, Keely was expecting their second child and after twenty-one hours of labour at the St John's Hospital in Santa Monica, Paris Beckett Brosnan was born at a little after 7 pm on Tuesday 27 February 2001. Both parents were delighted. 'He's a most beautiful baby,' Pierce announced, his broad smile more than enough to convey his obvious pride. Not only was Pierce present at the birth, he cut the umbilical cord and, according to Keely, actually held the baby before she did!

Though temporarily disengaged from the movie business, Brosnan had not been out of the news totally. There was the release of *The Tailor of Panama*, based on the John Le Carré story of lies and counter lies, in which he starred alongside Geoffrey

Rush and Jamie Lee Curtis, and after being becalmed for many long, tedious and almost despairing months, the seemingly impossible happened when *Grey Owl* finally went out on general release through Twentieth Century Fox.

Though firmly established in arguably the highest profile role in modern cinema, Brosnan continued to be his own man with a sure grasp on the kind of life he wants to lead, both on and off the screen. Since the mid 1990s he has given time, interest and personal involvement as an ambassador for The Prince's Trust. Formed by Prince Charles in 1976, The Prince's Trust aims to find challenge and adventure, combined with an element of service, for young people. After a faltering and hesitant start the Trust would eventually become a multi-million pound organization and the biggest independent charity of its kind in the country.

From his own childhood Brosnan knows enough about feeling isolated, not being one of the crowd, desperate for some self-esteem and confidence. As a youngster, he could easily have qualified for the challenge, adventure and help now provided by The Prince's Trust. Professionally, however, Brosnan's increasingly high profile owes almost everything to Bond. However, when the time comes for Pierce to call it a day on Bond, there are certain to be plenty of candidates keen to step into the 007 role. In fact pop star Robbie Williams moved in ahead of the pack by letting Eon Productions know the serious nature of his ambition. He told them he would be willing to take acting lessons and a year out from his music career to be the first Bond after Brosnan. And according to one or two industry insiders, Britain's Nigel Havers has serious ambitions to be a future Bond villain.

But for all the speculation about Brosnan's possible successor, Pierce continues to keep the industry guessing. As recently as December 1999 *Film Review* speculated on rumours that Brosnan had already been telling people that he would like to be the final James Bond, as well as the most financially successful – that he would still like to be there fighting overwhelming odds and coming up trumps and having fun while doing it, when James Bond finally ends his exploits on the silver screen. Yet only six months before, Pierce was forced to quash rumours that he was planning to give up the role because he was afraid of becoming typecast. Returning to Los Angeles in mid July 1999 he told the media: 'I don't know where these stories come from, but I'll be back as Bond. Doing these films is the best fun I've had in my life.'

Brosnan has doubtless already worked out that October 2002 will not only mark the fortieth anniversary of James Bond at the movies – four decades since Sean Connery was billed as a 'great new star' and Ursula Andress as the 'Bikini Honey' in *Dr No* – but also fifty years since Ian Fleming completed his first novel featuring James Bond, in 1952. What a wonderful opportunity for the biggest Bond/Brosnan bonanza of all time!

Pierce is said to be intelligent and astute, a thorough professional with high standards of performance. He thinks deeply about his roles and will often go to considerable lengths to achieve the right portrayal. He gives the impression of being easy-going, but attempt to take advantage of him and you're likely to find yourself in trouble. He is said to choose his friends carefully, is modest and withdrawn, loyal and genuine. He now appears confident, but it took a long time for that confidence to reach the surface. He was touched, delighted and flattered when his hometown of Navan in Ireland recently invited him over to receive the freedom of the town. 'It was lovely,' he said with obvious sincerity.

In the process of becoming what an increasing number of critics and cinemagoers feel to be the definitive Bond, he has also become internationally famous and exceedingly rich. He has even had his likeness depicted for the James Bond exhibit in London's Madame Tussaud's waxworks museum. Yet he is said to recognize the Bond circus for what it is, though respects its traditions and holds it in genuine affection.

The optimistic youth who, struck with ambition to become an actor, once attended a workshop in fire-eating while attending the Oval House Theatre Club in London and then became a chocolate tree in pantomime while working as acting assistant stage manager at the Theatre Royal in York, has cleared all the hurdles to achieve most, if not all, his professional ambitions. Privately, however, Pierce had important plans of his own to carry out in 2001. After his marriage to Keely Shaye-Smith had been twice postponed, as already mentioned when first his son Sean was involved in a serious road accident when a car in which he was travelling plunged over a cliff and then again when Keely was herself involved in a traffic incident, they were finally married on Saturday August 4, 2001 at Ballintubber Abbey, a thirteenth-century Catholic Church in County Mayo, Ireland. But in the end and despite various reports about the time and place, this was to be no hideaway marriage, no quiet elopement as many might have expected. One hundred and twenty close friends and family were there and the cost of the wedding was said to be as much as half a million pounds. Many of the guests, some of whom travelled from as far away as the United States and Australia, stayed at the beautiful Ashford Castle, where the reception was held. Keely was radiant and beautiful, Pierce smoothly tailored and handsome, and two gold rings, one for Pierce, one for Keely, were carried up the aisle by their four-year-old son Dylan. It was an outstandingly glamorous, glittering occasion; nothing less was good enough to seal Pierce's long-time love affair with Keely, though Brosnan would surprise, perhaps even shock, many of his fans by seemingly acting out of character in selling the exclusive rights to the wedding to *Hello* magazine, though he had earlier explained that only through some arrangement of this kind was he able to prevent jostling reporters and photographers from transforming this very special, personal occasion into a media circus. But the inside story eventually emerged that all monies received from the 'exploitation' of their marriage was destined for charitable causes.

Not long after the glamour and excitement of his wedding Brosnan was due to go before the cameras in the latest project from his own production company, Irish Dream Time – 'a marvellous family film' he explained – directed by Bruce Beresford – and shooting the next James Bond epic was scheduled to start in February 2002. It will be the twentieth adventure of the celebrated film hero and Brosnan was seen as the automatic choice to continue his success in the role for the fourth time. Against sporadic bouts of speculation about a possible successor, the studio insisted they had no plans to replace Brosnan. But the time must come when he relinquishes Bond, or Bond will cast off Brosnan. It is a time neither need fear, for despite their gigantic success together, each has proved strong enough to exist independently. Brosnan has always assiduously developed his life outside Bond and has proved his acting prowess as a man who, with apologies to Shakespeare, can play many parts and play them well. And as Pierce Brosnan once said: 'I want to be in acting for another fifty years.' Even his greatest fans could not wish for him to look further ahead than that.

Chronology

1953   Pierce Brendan Brosnan born (16 May) at Lourdes Maternity Home, Drogheda, County Lough, Ireland.

1959   Death of his maternal grandparents, with whom he lived, within a few months of each other.

1964   Moved to Putney, London, to live with his mother. Sees his first James Bond movie, *Goldfinger*, at the Odeon in Putney High Street when eleven years old.

1964   Attends Elliott Secondary School, Putney, for the first time on 8 September.

1969   Leaves Elliott School (25 July) two months after sixteenth birthday and begins work as a trainee commercial artist at a photographic studio in Putney.

1969   Joins the Oval House Theatre Group in London.

1970   Develops an increasing interest in acting.

1971   Visits London's Royal Court Theatre for a performance of *Antigone*, said to have been a major influence in developing his ambition to become a professional actor.

1973   Enrols for three-year drama course at the Drama Centre, Camden, London.

1976   Becomes an assistant stage manager at the Theatre Royal, York, on six-month contract.

1976   Makes first stage appearance at York (4–21 August) in *Wait Until Dark* by Frederick Knott.

1977   Appears in *The Red Devil Battery Sign* at the Round House, London, and later briefly at the Phoenix Theatre in London's West End.

1977   Appears on stage at Westcliffe-on-Sea, Essex, then secures a contract with the Citizens' Theatre, Glasgow.

1977   Appears in a production of *Filumena* by Italian director Franco Zeffirelli at the Lyric Theatre, London.

1978   Meets actress/model Cassandra Harris for the first time.

1979/80 First appearances on British television in Blood Sports (an episode of *The Professionals*) and The Carpathian Eagle (an episode of *The Hammer House of Horrors*).

1980   Returns to Westcliffe-on-Sea to appear in the award-winning play *Whose Life Is It Anyway?*

1980   Makes big-screen debut in *The Long Good Friday* and also appears in the film *The Mirror Crack'd*.

1980   Marries Cassandra Harris (27 December).

1982   Secures the role of Remington Steele (first episode screened in US in October) in long-running television series.

1983   Birth of son, Sean (September).

1986   Release of *Nomads*, his third film.

1986   Secures the role of James Bond to take over from Roger Moore, who retired, but loses the opportunity because of contractual commitments (*Remington Steele*).

1987   Appears with Michael Caine in *The Fourth Protocol* (his fourth film).

1987   Final episode of *Remington Steele* screened (February).

1987   Cassandra (Cassie) officially diagnosed (December) as suffering from ovarian cancer.

1988   Takes central role in TV mini-series called *Noble House*.

1988   Appears in two further films, *Taffin* and *The Deceivers*, his fifth and sixth films.

1989   Arranges surprise birthday party at London's Savoy Hotel for Cassie's two children (with Dermot Harris) Charlotte, 18 and Christopher, 17.

1991   Appears in *Mr Johnson*, his seventh film.

1991   Cassie enters a cancer hospital in Los Angeles (2 December).

1991   Cassie dies in hospital on Saturday, 28 December.

1992   Appears in *Live Wire*, his eighth film.

1992   Stars in *The Lawnmower Man*, his ninth film to be released and his first to become a major box-office success.

1993   Appears in *Entangled*, his tenth film.

1994   Appears in *Mrs Doubtfire* and *Love Affair*, his eleventh and twelfth films.

1994   Meets Keely Shaye-Smith (environmental journalist) for the first time.

1994   Hears officially (1 June) that he is to be the new James Bond, taking over from Timothy Dalton.

1995   Stars in *GoldenEye* (released in November) as the new James Bond.

1996   Announced (June) that Keely was pregnant.

1997   Present at the birth of his son Dylan Thomas (Monday, 13 January).

1997   Appears in three films: *The Mirror Has Two Faces* (with Barbra Streisand), *Mars Attacks!* (with Jack Nicholson and Glenn Close) and he stars in *Dante's Peak* (in the leading role alongside Linda Hamilton).

1997   Stars in his sixteenth film, his biggest box-office attraction of the year and his second as James Bond, in *Tomorrow Never Dies*.

1998   Stars in *The Nephew*, a film made by Irish Dream Time (his own production company in partnership with business associate Beau St Clair). He is also the film's producer. The picture shown exclusively on Sky Movies.

1998   Working on location in Canada, making *Grey Owl*, the story of eco-warrior Archie Belaney.

1999   Stars in *The Thomas Crown Affair* with co-star Rene Russo. He also produced the film, along with Beau St Clair.

1999   Over the years has helped raise more than £3 million for women's health research.

1999   Stars as James Bond for the third time in *The World Is Not Enough*, co-starring with Sophie Marceau, Robert Carlyle, Denise Richards, Dame Judi Dench, Samantha Bond, Desmond Llewelyn and Robbie Coltrane.

2000   Marriage to Keely Shaye-Smith was twice put on hold when first Sean suffered complications following a serious car crash and then Keely was involved in a less serious road accident.

2000   Continues to give significant time and support to Prince Charles' The Prince's Trust.

2000   Turned down film offers to spend quality time with Keely.

2000   In early summer Keely was expecting their second child.

2000   After considerable delay *Grey Owl* is released.

2001   Second child, Paris Beckett, born on 27 February.

2001   Stars in *The Tailor of Panama* with Geoffrey Rush and Jamie Lee Curtis.

2001   Married to Keely Shaye-Smith on Saturday, August 4 at a glittering occasion held in Ireland at Ballintubber Abbey with reception at Ashford Castle.

2002   Expected to star as special agent 007 for the fourth time when the next James Bond movie is due to begin shooting in February.

Filmography

The Long Good Friday (1980)
Directed by John Mackenzie; produced by Barry Hanson.
Appeared towards the bottom of the cast list in a movie that starred Bob Hoskins and Helen Mirren and also featured Dave King, Bryan Marshall, Eddie Constantine and Stephen Davis.

The Mirror Crack'd (1980)
Directed by Guy Hamilton; produced by John Brabourne.
Appeared towards the bottom of the cast list in a movie that starred Angela Lansbury, Geraldine Chaplin, Elizabeth Taylor, Rock Hudson, Tony Curtis, Edward Fox, Kim Novak and Derek Thompson.

Nomads (1986)
Directed by John McTiernan; produced by George Pappas.
Appeared with Lesley Anne-Down and Adam Ant.

The Fourth Protocol (1987)
Directed by John Mackenzie; produced by Timothy Burrill.
Appeared with Michael Caine, Joanna Cassidy, Ned Beatty, Ray McAnally, Ian Richardson and Betsy Brantley.

Taffin (1988)
Directed by Francis Megahy; produced by William Alexander.

Appeared with Alison Doody, Ray McAnally, Jeremy Child and Patrick Bergin.

The Deceivers (1988)
Directed by Nicholas Meyer; produced by Michael White.
Appeared with Saeed Jaffrey, Shashi Kapoor, Helena Michell, Keith Michell and David Robb.

Mister Johnson (1991)
Directed by Bruce Beresford; produced by Michael Fitzgerald.
Appeared with Edward Woodward, Maynard Eziashi and Denis Quilley.

Live Wire (1992)
Directed by Christopher Duguay; produced by Brett Leonard.
Appeared with Ron Silver, Ben Cross and Lisa Eibacher.

The Lawnmower Man (1992)
Directed by Brett Leonard; produced by Gimel Everett.
Appeared with Jeff Fahey and Jenny Wright.

Entangled (1993)
Directed by Max Fischer; produced by Max Fischer.
Appeared with Judd Nelson and Laurence Treil.

Mrs Doubtfire (1994)
Directed by Chris Columbus; produced by Robin Williams and Marsha Garces Williams.
Appeared with Robin Williams, Sally Field, Harvey Fierstein and Robert Prosky.

Love Affair (1994)
Directed by Glenn Gordon Caron; produced by Warren Beatty.

Appeared with Warren Beatty, Annette Bening, Katherine Hepburn, Gary Shandling, Kate Capshaw and Chloe Webb.

GoldenEye (1995)
Directed by Martin Campbell; produced by Michael G. Wilson and Barbara Broccoli.
Appeared with Sean Bean, Izabella Scorupco, Famke Janssen, Joe Don Baker, Dame Judi Dench, Robbie Coltrane, Tcheky Karyo, Gottfried John, Alan Cumming, Desmond Llewelyn and Samantha Bond.

The Mirror Has Two Faces (1997)
Directed by Barbra Streisand; produced by Barbra Streisand and Arnon Michan.
Appeared with Barbra Streisand, Jeff Bridges and Lauren Bacall.

Mars Attacks! (1997)
Directed by Tim Burton; produced by Tim Burton and Larry Franco.
Appeared with Jack Nicholson, Glenn Close, Annette Bening, Danny DeVito, Michael J. Fox, Lukas Haas, Sarah Jessica Parker, Martin Short and Tom Jones.

Dante's Peak (1997)
Directed by Roger Donaldson; produced by Gale Anne Hurd and Joseph M. Singer.
Appeared with Linda Hamilton.

Tomorrow Never Dies (1997)
Directed by Roger Spottiswoode; produced by Michael G. Wilson and Barbara Broccoli.
Appeared with Jonathan Pryce, Michelle Yeoh, Teri Hatcher, Ricky Jay, Gotz Otto, Joe Don Baker, Vincent Schiavelli, Dame Judi

Dench, Desmond Llewelyn, Samantha Bond, Colin Salmon, Geoffrey Palmer, Julian Fellowes, Terence Rigby and Cecilie Thomsen.

The Nephew (1998)
Directed by Eugene Brady; produced by Pierce Brosnan.
Appeared with Donal McCann and Hill Harper.

The Thomas Crown Affair (1999)
Directed by John McTiernan; produced by Pierce Brosnan and Beau St Clair.
Appeared with Renne Russo, Denis Leary, Ben Gazzara, Frankie Faison, Fritz Weaver, Charles Keating, Mark Margolis and Faye Dunaway.

The World Is Not Enough (1999)
Directed by Michael Apted; produced by Michael G. Wilson and Barbara Broccoli.
Appeared with Sophie Marceau, Robert Carlyle, Denise Richards, Dame Judi Dench, Samantha Bond, Desmond Llewelyn, John Cleese and Robbie Coltrane.

Grey Owl (2000)
Directed by Richard Attenborough; produced by Jake Eberts and Richard Attenborough.
Appeared with Anne Galipeau, Renie Asherson and Stephanie Cole.

The Tailor of Panama (2001)
Directed by John Boorman; produced by John Boorman.
Appeared with Geoffrey Rush and Jamie Lee Curtis.

Index

Entries in italics refer to films unless otherwise indicated

221